# Questions

## and

# Answers

## on

# Creation/Evolution

John N. Moore

**Baker Book House**
**Grand Rapids, Michigan**

*First printing, January 1977*
*Second printing, April 1978*
*Third printing, October 1980*
*Fourth printing, November 1981*

Copyright © 1976 by Baker Book House Company
ISBN: 0-8010-5997-6
Printed in the United States of America

# Contents

# Illustrations and Charts

# Foreword

This book contains answers to questions raised at the conclusion of numerous lectures, seminars, and special classes that I have presented in the last few years. I have not attempted, however, an exhaustive treatment of the multifaceted subject areas involved in the creation/evolution controversy. My answers are meant primarily as aids to nonscience readers—students, parents, and pastors who are called upon to answer similar questions. In this way I hope to put "legs to the concept" of brotherly love—that many might be strengthened in their faith in God, and that all readers might be led to think more deeply on these matters.

These questions and answers are arranged to follow the three main phases of the great creative acts of Almighty God. As given in the Bible, God's creative work commenced with the beginning of the universe, continued with the creation of life, and was climaxed in the sixth day of the creative week with the appearance of humankind.

It is most appropriate that human beings, who are continuously curious about themselves and their environment, should ask questions. To ask questions is entirely scriptural. Paul, for example, urged the Thessalonians to prove all things and hold fast to that which is good. And Paul advised Timothy to study to be approved unto God that he might rightly divide the Word of truth. In turn, there is good logic for Christians to prepare for rightly dividing the ideas of other men and women. Also, Job indicated that all things are included in the rightful study of the Christian: "But ask now the beasts, and they shall teach thee; and the fowls of the air, and they shall tell thee; ... and the fishes of the sea shall declare unto thee. Who knoweth not in all these that the hand of the Lord hath wrought this?" (12:7-9).

Chapter 1 contains inquiries collected under the question, What is science? We live in the "Scientific Age," and we must understand science. A particularly useful and very special glossary of terms is included. Chapter 2 deals with the question, What is evolution?, beginning with important definitions and considering evidences. The important question of time is treated in chapter 3, which is on dating methods. Evolutionists must have a great expanse of time in their formulations. Creationist scientists, however, are able to present careful reasons why the universe, and hence the earth, might very well be quite young. Regardless of the question of time there seems to be no doubt that immense changes have occurred on the earth's surface, and such changes are the subject of the questions in chapter 4. In biblical sequence, the next three chapters contain representative questions that are commonly raised by people who want to know about the origins of the universe, life, and humankind. The focus of the last chapter is on the extensive impact of evolutionary thinking or "evolutionism" across the full range of man's disciplines of knowledge.

# Introduction

What can be said to those who will not consider the Bible as the source of creation ideas? When they raise their questions in public assemblages I make my position clear by answering these three questions: (1) Is the Bible historically authentic?, (2) Is there a conflict between Genesis 1 and Genesis 2 as to the order of creation?, and (3) Are there any scientific errors in the Bible?

1. *Is the Bible historically authentic?* Because of multitudinous archaeological findings, it is now possible to hold fast to the position that the New Testament is historically accurate. It was written by men who knew Jesus Christ firsthand and on face to face encounter. The reader is directed to explanations of the fully historic nature of the New Testament *and* the Old Testament in such works as: *History and Christianity* by John Warwick Montgomery, *Genesis and Archaeology* by Howard F. Vos (or *An Introduction to Bible Archaeology* by Vos), and *A Scientific Investigation of the Old Testament* by Robert Dick Wilson. Specialists have gained historic support for biblical events as far back as Genesis 14 wherein reference is made to the King's Highway; and the names such as Nahor, Serug, and Terah in Genesis 11 are close to names of archaeological mound sites under investigation in this decade.

There is no need for anyone today to feel the slightest necessity of giving credance to still repeated claims that Moses could not have written the Pentateuch because there was no writing in his day, that the Hittite people did not exist and were "invented" by the Bible author, or that Abraham was only an uneducated nomad. Archaeologists and language specialists have already demolished such claims, since they know now that there was writing long before Moses, that clear evidence of the Hittites has been found, and that schools and libraries existed in the city of Ur (the birthplace of Abraham).

There are those who feel mention should be made of the beliefs on origins of people of the Islamic faith, or Eastern religions, or Pacific islanders, or other natives around the world. In response I usually point out that beliefs on origins of all other people have been derived from the Israelite-Hebrew tradition passed orally for many generations and presented finally by Moses in Genesis. This position can be documented in scholarly research, but such study is beyond the scope of this book.

2. *Is there a conflict between Genesis 1 and Genesis 2 as to the order of creation?* So often a claim of conflict between Genesis 1 and Genesis 2 is heard from those reluctant to accept the authenticity of the Bible. As well as I can understand the situation, there is no substance to a claim of such conflict. I feel Genesis 1 was written that we might know of past events that occurred before there were any human beings on the earth. No one would know of such unchanging answers about beginnings of the universe and all that is therein without the revelation contained in Genesis 1.

Then what about Genesis 2 in which the order of appearance of living things does not follow that contained in Genesis 1? Again, as well as I can understand the situation, the purpose for writing Genesis 2 was different from that of Genesis 1. In the second chapter, basic points on the relationship between God (the Creator) and humankind (the created) are made evident. In Genesis 2, therefore, attention to the order of creation events is subordinated to the explanation of how God provided a pleasant natural environment for man, how God provided woman as companion and mate for man, and how God ordained the state of marriage.

3. *Are there any scientific errors in the Bible?* A commonly heard expression is, "The Bible is not a scientific textbook." That is true, for the Bible was written for a different purpose. Never-

theless, the Bible contains many references to the natural environment and to natural processes. Biblical authors did not write in the terminology of modern physical and biological sciences since they wrote in everyday language understandable to their readers. Yet wherever the biblical writers touched on subject areas studied today by scientists they were amazingly accurate. There are no scientific errors or mistakes in the Bible. Dr. Henry M. Morris has discussed this matter at some length in his book *Many Infallible Proofs* (pp. 241–245). Dr. Morris cites numerous passages of the Bible, which he has listed under the headings of hydrology, geology, astronomy, meteorology, biology, and physics.

*John N. Moore*
*East Lansing, Michigan*

# 1

# What Is Science?

## PURPOSE AND ACTIVITIES OF SCIENTISTS

### What is science?

There are many definitions of science. However, the two main aspects of the scientific endeavor are (1) identification and collection of information, plus (2) the essential methods or procedures by which information is gained.

Following are a number of definitions of science:

> Science can be described as consisting of two forms: (a) science is a body of useful and practical knowledge and a method of obtaining it; (b) science is pure intellectual activity. *N. Campbell, 1952.*

> Science is knowledge of the natural world obtained by sense interaction with that world. *R. H. Bube, 1967.*

> Science is all knowledge collected by means of the scientific method, where scientific method is the cycle of induction, deduction, verification and eternal search for improvement of theories which are only tentatively held. *J. G. Kemany, 1959.*

> Science is that mode of inquiry which attempts to arrive at knowledge of the world by the method of observation and by the method of confirmed hypothesis on what is given in observation. *A. C. Benjamin, 1965.*

> Science is the ordered knowledge of natural phenomena and the rational study of the relations between the concepts

in which these phenomena are expressed. *W. C. Dampier, 1961.*

Science is the body of knowledge obtained by methods based upon the authority of observation. *R. B. Fischer, 1975.*

Science is a branch of study which is concerned either with a connected body of demonstrated truths or with observed facts systematically classified and more or less colligated by being brought under general laws, and which includes trustworthy methods for the discovery of new truth within its own domain. *Oxford Dictionary.*

Science is an interconnected series of concepts and conceptual schemes that have developed as a result of experimentation and observation and are fruitful of further experimentation and observations. *J. B. Conant, 1951.*

The important distinction between science and those other systematizations is that science is self-testing and self-correcting. The testing and correcting are done by means of observations that can be repeated with essentially the same results by normal persons operating by the same methods and with the same approach. *G. G. Simpson, 1961.*

## What is the prime purpose of scientists?

Not all scientists have the same goals or purposes. Some scientists study limited problems and seek immediate answers. Albert Einstein even sought a completely unified system of scientific knowledge, which he never reached.

Nevertheless, the prime purpose of scientists "in the long run" is the development of explanations of aspects of the natural environment. Such explanations are usually called scientific theories, such as the gene theory, the atomic theory, and the kinetic-molecular theory.

## What are the tools of scientists?

Both biological scientists and physical scientists use a fantastic array of tools, instruments, measurement devices, and utensils of research that have been developed as modern technology has increased.

For example, besides simple rulers, yardsticks, calipers, or the stethoscopes used by family doctors, microscopes, telescopes, radio telescopes, electroscopes, spectroscopes, betatrons, cyclotrons, and radioactively "tagged" chemicals are but a small sampling of the vast instrumentation used by scientists.

All these tools mentioned are specific means for making observations, directly or indirectly, about aspects of the natural environment of humankind on earth and in space. By these means data, facts, or information are gained that would not be known if scientists had to rely on their unaided senses of perception. All such tools extend scientists' ability to perceive things.

## What are the various scientific activities?

Though the activities or varieties of methods employed by scientists are many and often quite complex, all activities of scientists may be grouped under two headings: *empirical* (a special inclusive term for methods of observation) and *theoretical* (a special inclusive term for explanations and scientific theories by which scientists unify and correlate observations). A brief way of summarizing scientific activities is to state objectives of good science instruction and inquiry in science as involving *process skills,* such as:

1. Observing
2. Making operational definitions
3. Classifying
4. Inferring
5. Forming questions and hypotheses
6. Predicting
7. Measuring
8. Experimenting
9. Interpreting data
10. Communicating
11. Formulating models
12. Re-examining

On the following page is a listing of various methods used by scientists in their observational (empirical) work and the main parts of their theoretical formulations. In Appendices Two and Three the terms are then defined, followed by examples of both empirical and theoretical aspects of scientific activities.

# ASPECTS OF SCIENTIFIC ACTIVITIES

**Empirical**

Observations (including initial or prior observations)—recorded awarenesses

Descriptions

Classification—grouping, ordering

Calculations—numerical manipulations

Problems—questions

Hypotheses—testable
(tentative answers)

Analogy

Inductive
reasoning

Controlled
Experimentation

(testing)

Trial
and
Error

Generalizations—laws

Predictions—testable
(if . . . then)

(Experimental
assumptions)

Deductive
reasoning

- - - - - - - - - - - - - - - - - - - - - - - - - - - - - - - - - - - - - -

Scientific theory (Theoretical model) (Conceptual scheme)

Theoretical assumptions—imaginary aspect (object or event)
(list of postulates)

atom
molecule
gene

Theorems—deductive reasoning
(predictions)

**Theoretical**

---

FOUNDATIONAL, BASIC ASSUMPTIONS (or PRESUPPOSITONS)

a. Objectivity of study
b. Cause and effect
c. Testability of ideas
d. Objects/events outside of observers
e. Uniformity of natural environment

## Are there any limiting principles for scientific work?

Yes. These are amply represented in the work by great physical scientists who began modern science and by leading biological scientists as well. Since modern science began with the work of Galileo, Kepler, Newton, Linnaeus, Ray, Clerk-Maxwell, Faraday, Pasteur, and Virchow, it should be noted that these men were all theists. They believed that the universe and this earth were created by God, and that they, as created in the image of God, had abilities for observation, search, and reasoning whereby they could learn about this earth and the universe.

Because modern science was begun as a venture to "think God's thoughts after Him" (as Kepler expressed the thought), created men were limited by their abilities. In hindsight, we can accurately say that these early scientists limited themselves by emphasizing their scientific work as—

1. *empirical,* that is, observational. They studied things in their environment and used tools and measurements to extend their observing ability.

2. *quantitative,* that is, based upon measurement of changes of objects in their environment. They deliberately altered or moved objects so as to measure change or aspects of relationships of objects. The physical scientists especially set the style, so to speak, in always seeking to gain careful measurements, in terms such as length, weight, volume, and density.

3. *mechanical,* that is, these scientists sought to represent the order and patterns of things they found around them. In some cases they produced physical models of what they were studying; in other instances they prepared orderly lists and stated divisions and subdivisions of classifications of objects and events.

4. *corrective,* that is, under repeated examination and re-examination errors could be detected and the same results could be gained and compared time after time. Through such steps they were able to arrive at certain lawful relationships of objects and of events.

From the standpoint of careful continuance of these limiting principles, many scholars in approximately the last 150 years have changed these principles into *dogmas*. Therefore: (a) *Empiricism* is emphasized according to the viewpoint that the only or proper source of information is scientific methodology and intuition and revelation are completely ignored or discarded (this position is also known as scientism); (b) *Materialism* is emphasized in accordance with the viewpoint that matter is the primary reality and that spiritual aspects of human existence are not important; (c) *Determinism* is emphasized according to the viewpoint that all events, including human behavior, are controlled by impersonal forces; and (d) *Utopianism* is stressed to push forward the thought that human beings can be self-corrective enough to bring about an ideal society (today this "hope" is fostered in the public schools through an almost exclusive presentation of total evolutionism, whereby supposedly the climax of "evolutionary" change will result in perfection with God [according to teachings of Pierre Teilhard de Chardin]).

## What do scientists do when they encounter contradictions between their research findings and their scientific theories?

Actually, scientists are most reluctant to change their basic ideas. Consequently, when certain isolated results are reported that are different than expected, most scientists will take steps to adhere to the ideas held by the majority of scientists. The following list contains several of the common steps scientists follow when faced with contradictions between their research findings and their scientific theories:

1. Almost invariably, the first step is to *ignore the contradictions*. After all, the difficulty usually involves only a part of the theory in question. Therefore, the contradiction may be of limited importance, and further research may resolve the difficulty. Suspended judgement is practiced.

2. A *claim of error* of research method or interpretation of findings is often heard. The author of the report of contradictory evidence is usually charged with carelessness or inaccuracy.

3. If repeated reports sustain the condition of real and

vital contradictions then the relevant *part of the scientific theory may be modified.* Note that such action is taken only after *repeated* analysis results in the same information and an acceptable alteration of the existing theory can be developed.

4. Another possible avenue of approach to contradictions is to *develop a completely alternative theory* along with research implications and ramifications that can be developed regarding both theories. In other words, two scientific theories are allowed to "coexist," as was the case while physicists considered light as both wave phenomena and particles in motion (a difference which apparently has been resolved mathematically in recent years).

5. The history of science contains many examples where a *new theory completely replaced another theory,* as when Mendelian genetics replaced the blending theory of inheritance, or the particulate theory of electricity replaced the fluid electrical theory.

## What are the laws of science?

These are broad statements of the relationship of observed (directly or indirectly) aspects of the natural environment. They are, therefore, well-supported descriptive statements about atoms, molecules, genes, elements, charges, planets, and gases, to mention some of the aspects that are specifically described in the laws of attraction and repulsion, planetary motion, definite proportion, gaseous molecules, Mendelian genetics, and thermodynamics.

## EVIDENCE AND FAITH

### What is conclusive evidence?

When the scientist supports a conclusion with data gained from direct or indirect measurements, and he has checked and rechecked his results, he usually feels that his evidence is conclusive. Conclusive evidence is that type of evidence about which only one conclusion can be made.

## What is circumstantial evidence?

Circumstantial evidence is that type of evidence about which more than one conclusion might be stated. In other words, the conclusion made is based solely on the circumstances. Such circumstances might be seen by one observer from one angle (on which he bases his conclusion) and by another observer from another angle (resulting in a different conclusion).

Often, conclusions based on circumstantial evidence are conclusions or decisions made about conditions that cannot be repeated. Thus conclusions that some geologists reach about events that occurred on the surface of the earth in the past are based on circumstantial evidence—evidence that cannot be repeated. In general, evolutionists make conclusions about the origin of physical characteristics on circumstances that they find but cannot repeat. Their conclusions are based solely on these circumstances, and they cannot explain in fully scientific manner how the circumstances that they observe ever come into existence.

## Is the scientific process based on faith?

Scientific activities are not based on faith in the commonly used religious sense of the word as found in Hebrews 11:1—that faith is the substance of things hoped for, the evidence of things not seen. But, to the degree that scientists believe that real objects exist in the natural environment, that events in the natural environment occur with some uniform regularity, and that observable effects are due to some specific cause or causes, then we can say that the scientist has "faith" in these relationships. He assumes that the same conditions, in the main, will occur day after day, that he can repeat certain experiments and gain reliable measurements. These are the "given" conditions upon which scientific activities are completed and in which the scientist has "faith."

## How do you relate scientific activities with the acceptance of something by faith?

This question is similar to the previous question. The term

"faith" in this question likely involves some religious meaning, that is, faith in God the Creator.

There is no necessary conflict. Many leading scientists, such as Kepler, Clerk-Maxwell, and Pasteur were sincere believers in God as Creator, and they were most successful scientists. Some historians would claim that these men were successful scientists because they had faith that the heavens and the earth were framed by the Word of God; they had faith that God had given them abilities to think God's thoughts after Him to some extent.

Faith in God is not incompatible with success in science. This is evident in the lives of many contemporary scientists.

## SCIENTIFIC REASONING AND WRITING

### What are some "tests" for scientific thinking?

Scientific thinking is similar to our everyday thinking. By this I mean that logical thought is practiced by every human being. Scientists, however, have developed special patterns for detailed application to their specific areas of research and study.

Thus scientific thinking is characterized as being based on direct or indirect observation. Observations are then repeated and repeated until detailed descriptions and classifications of data plus experimentation are possible as means of double-checking initial observations. A most striking characteristic of scientific thinking is the practice of developing scientific theories that might be recognized according to the following criteria*:

1. A good theory can be used to correlate many separate facts, especially important *prior observations,* into a logical framework of thought.

2. During continued use of a theory *new relations* are realized and further steps for research are suggested.

3. From a good theory *predictions* can be deduced *that are testable* through direct experience.

---

*Modified from Chapter 8, "On the Nature of Scientific Theory" in *Foundations of Modern Physical Science* by Gerald Holton and Duane H. D. Roller. Reading, Mass.: Addison-Wesley Publishing Co., Inc. 1958.

4. A successful theory will be based upon a *few basic assumptions* or postulates.

5. A good theory is flexible enough that *modifications* can be made where needed.

### Are there any criteria for scientific writing?

The non-specialist particularly asks this question and, in so doing, reflects a natural inquiry in these days of both increasing technological advancements *and* broadly disseminated reports of speculations and conjectures about extraterrestrial life, genetic human engineering, and other "charged" topics.

Commonly, the words used about topics such as these are a good means for noting the storytelling or scenario–play writing aspects of an author trying to communicate his ideas about what "could," "would," "supposedly," "possibly," "probably," or "might" come to pass. These terms are used heavily in speculative, conjectural writing that can readily be contrasted with careful scientific writing.

In scientifically written material, the reader can expect to find these main sections (not necessarily in this order): (1) initial observations and statement of a problem or perplexity for which an answer can reasonably be sought; (2) a review of scientific literature for summary of any similar research reports and a listing of relevant findings that might be useful in the current problem area of research; (3) statement of a hypothesis, or tentative answer to the problem presented—and even some mention of possible alternative answers that could be checked out if the problem seems to have several facets or aspects that could be studied in separate but related parts; (4) description of the methods, materials, and equipment used in the research on the primary hypothesis and any corollary answers to various related aspects of the problem; (5) report of results; (6) discussion of the results; and (7) summary and conclusions, and often mention of further problems that became evident as the research was completed.

Clearly there is a characteristic format of careful scientific writing. Absence of such a format with most, if not all, of the stated elements means the reader has a specific basis for considering such deficient writing as mostly speculative and conjectural, and not an example of good, careful scientific writing.

Speculations and scenarios about the origin of the universe, origin of first life on the earth, existence of extraterrestrial life, and origin of humankind are *not* examples of proper scientific writing.

## Do any of the Bible authors illustrate scientific thinking or writing?

To the extent that the first four books of the New Testament are essentially eyewitness reports, the reader knows that objectivity and care of description of real people and events is involved.

As linguistic and archaeological research continues, more and more corroboration of the Old Testament as far back as Genesis 14 has accumulated. Thus the Bible authors wrote objectively accurate accounts of what they saw just as scientists report their scientific research. The Bible authors generally showed the same assumption of cause and effect and uniformity of natural events as is characteristic of scientists' reports. Miracles are described by biblical authors in a manner that provides the reader with firsthand reports of how God momentarily altered or modified the usually uniform state of things as mentioned in Genesis 8:22: "While the earth remaineth, seedtime and harvest, and cold and heat, and summer and winter, and day and night shall not cease." (In fact, it is only because miracles are not repeatable that scientists are unable to study them. Scientists therefore cannot deny miracles, but only admit that miracles are outside their area of research and study.)

## Is the Genesis account of creation scientific? Is evolution scientific?

According to specific characteristics of scientific thinking and writing, neither the Genesis account of creation nor evolution ("molecules to man") are scientific.

No observations by a professionally trained scientist were ever made of either the events contained in the Genesis account of creation or written expressions about grand scale evolution. Therefore, modern scientists are in the same position as Job with regard to first origins. Macro- or megaevolution\* is without any foundation in observational science, and hence is not scientific.

Obviously, the beginning of the universe, the start of life on the earth, and the appearance of the first human beings cannot be repeated. Yet repeated observations, made directly or indirectly, are the very basis of scientific work. Human beings would know nothing about first origins in any unchanging form if they did not have revelation from the Creator as provided in Genesis. Evolutionary thinking is essentially offered, consciously or unconsciously, as a substitute for answers on first origins given in the Genesis account. Generally, evolutionists have invented their schemes because they will not accept answers contained in the Genesis account of creation.

### Since creation and evolution ideas about first origins are not scientific theories, should either be presented in the science class?

Strictly speaking, a course or curriculum centered properly on scientific activities would not contain any treatment of first origins. This is an ideal situation, however, since scientists and science educators will not desist from discussion of first origins.

Therefore, in a pluralistic society, I hold that only one course is open for educators in the public schools. They can no longer continue presentation of the favored evolutionary ideas, and they are duty-bound in the context of full academic freedom and responsibility and in accountability to taxpaying parents to present *both* the evolution model and the creation model about first origins.

Educators in parochial schools can ill afford to omit treatment of evolution if they accept the responsibility of preparing their students to be in the world but not of the world. Only by fully

---

\*Megaevolution is change *between* kinds of organisms, compared to microevolution, which is change *within* kinds of organisms.

understanding both the creation account of origins with a sound scientific basis *and* the evolutionists' attempt to explain first origins, however, will students of parochial schools be prepared to meet ideas regarding first origins.

# 2

# What Is Evolution? What Is Creation?

## EVOLUTION AND CREATION MODELS

### What is the evolution model*?

Because different meanings are often associated with the term *evolution*, complete consensus on the evolution model might be very hard to establish. Nevertheless, in this context evolution is understood to mean "molecules to man," to use one textbook subtitle expression, and therefore is not used to designate just any degree or kind of change, such as change of genetic frequencies or genetic variation within some recognizable kind of plant or animal. Actually the "molecules to man" thesis of modern evolutionists involves stellar evolution, molecular evolution, organic evolution, and social (societal) evolution, which all may be summarized under the terms *total evolution* or *grand scale evolution*.

The evolution model is an explanatory belief system based upon eternal existence of matter from which have come an ascending series of elements by nucleogenesis, changes by stellar evolution of "young" stars into "old" stars, galaxies, and planets (especially the earth with life that appeared spontaneously

---

*When reference is made to ideas about first origins, the term *model* rather than *theory* is preferable today. Therefore quotation marks should always be used in such designations as big bang "theory," steady state "theory," or continuous creation "theory," so as to denote a difference between ideas men have about first origins and well-grounded scientific theories, such as the atomic theory, the nuclear theory, the kinetic-molecular theory, or the gene theory.

through molecular evolution followed by organic evolution, including human evolution).

In summary, evolutionists' ideas have to do with *origination* of order out of disorder and *integration* of more complex patterns out of least complex patterns.

## Does the term *evolution* merely mean change?

To say that evolution merely means change is not acceptable to creationist scientists. Of course this is one meaning, along with "an unfolding," that will be found in an unabridged dictionary.

Everyone should clearly understand, however, that modern evolutionists use the term *evolution* to mean that all the varieties of living things, including human beings, have had a common ancestry with a single cell, which they believe was formed after molecules combined to form protein materials.

Evolution, then, is most properly summarized in the phrase, "molecules to man."

## What is the source of men's ideas about evolution?

Evolution was not "invented" or originated by Charles Darwin. The concept of common ancestry of all varieties of living things today and in the past from a single cell began in the minds of Greek thinkers many centuries before Darwin. Evolution is a pre-Christian idea. Of course, first origin ideas of the Greeks did not show the same pattern of organization found in the writings of Maupertuis, Buffon, Diderot, Kant, Lamarck, and Darwin of the eighteenth and nineteenth centuries.

Actually, at the time that Charles Darwin's book *The Origin of Species* was published the majority of scientists believed in the first origin of all things by special creative acts of the Creator God. As young scientists and certain leading theologians read Darwin's book, however, they became persuaded to his position. He provided just the type of plausible line of reasoning that made evolution intellectually acceptable. As historians mention in their reports and analyses, many "converts" were made to a belief in the origin of living things separate from acts of God.

# THE EVOLUTION MODEL AND THE CREATION MODEL COMPARED

| Statements of Evolutionary Uniformitarianism Model of Origins (based upon world-view of naturalism) | Statements of Catastrophism and Creationism Model of Origins (based upon world-view of theism) |
|---|---|
| 1. Matter has existed eternally (no cause)<br>a. Matter continually appears (from energy?)<br>b. Matter exploded and continues to expand. | 1. Universe was created essentially in present state. (Cause: Eternal Creator)<br>a. Matter, planets, stars created complete.<br>b. Light rays created directly. |
| 2. A whole series of elements was generated (evolved); and stars, planets have evolved by accretion. | 2. Universe was created complete and basically stable. |
| 3. Apparent land features resulted from specific causes of vulcanism, diastrophism, gradation (the present is the key to the past). | 3. Causes seen in present were not causes of land features (the present is only the key to the present). |
| 4. Forces of origination and integration exist. | 4. Catastrophism, decay and conservational activities prevail in antagonism. |
| 5. Geologic column is evidence of vast "history" of the earth. | 5. Only local sedimentary columns exist and worldwide destruction is evidenced by worldwide distribution of sedimentary rocks. |
| 6. Because of innate propensity of matter, organic matter came from inorganic matter by spontaneous generation. | 6. Since spontaneous generation of life is contradictory to Second Law of Thermodynamics, only special creation of life could be cause of life. |
| 7. Changes in evolutionary sequence of life forms are due to random mutational changes in genes. | 7. Mutations are evidence of increased disorder (entropy) and only changes *within* limits of kinds, group, or species result from mutations/recombination of genes. |
| 8. Changes of complex forms or kinds from less complex kinds are the result of accumulation of random variations. | 8. Conservative processes are involved in operation of genetic code resulting in essential stability (fixity) of basic kinds, groups, species, with no accumulation of random variations. |
| 9. Mankind is related to the ape through an unknown common ancestor. | 9. Mankind is a special creation. |
| 10. Fossils of genus *Homo* are immediate ancestors of modern man. | 10. "Ape-like" features of prehistoric man may be due to disease and degeneration. |
| 11. Races of man resulted from mutations and segregation in early man-like forms. | 11. Human beings all belong to one race and languages are merely tribal differences. |
| 12. Evolutionary humanism can be a guiding faith. | 12. Alienation, identity, and relevance can be answered in context of relation to Creator God. |

## What is the creation model?

Consensus on the creation model might be difficult to reach since the term *creation* can refer to the acts of God as Creator and/or to the sum total of, or the end results of, His creation work. Thus God alone is properly the subject of the verb *create* as far as first origins is concerned. But modern scientists are able to research the creation, that is, the fullness of the natural environment of humankind, which today necessarily includes the seas and surface of the earth, the atmosphere of the earth, much of the solar system, and even beyond—as telescopes and other tools of modern technology are employed to study aspects of the universe.

The creation model is an explanatory belief system based upon the existence of an eternal Creator who established a complete, finished, and functional universe in all aspects regarding elements, galaxies, stars, and planets (especially the earth with mutually exclusive groups of plants and animals).

## What is the source of men's ideas about creation?

Today there are many sources for ideas about the creation of the universe, life on the earth, and humankind. Sacred and classical writings of the Moslems, Chinese, and Indians and the traditions of Pacific Islanders, American Indians, and other peoples too numerous to mention, refer to first things. Moreover, excellent modern scholarship and research regarding clay tablets, papyrus scrolls, and multiple languages of the peoples of the world are basic to the generalization that all the above-mentioned sources of ideas on first origins are essentially derivative of the Israelite-Hebrew tradition, which is the most ancient of all.

Of course, the Israelite-Hebrew tradition has long been available for study and research. Therefore other scientists and myself have maintained for several years that the only source of unchanging and unchangeable answers about the origin of the universe, life on the earth, and humankind are those of the Israelite-Hebrew tradition as provided in the first book of the Torah, the Book of Genesis in the Bible.

**How do evolutionists define the term *species*?**

This is a difficult term to define. It was a source of difficulty for Charles Darwin and Sir Julian Huxley, and remains a problem for modern biologists. One could say almost facetiously that *species* means whatever a group of authorities says that it means. The term *species*, however, is usually used to refer to some group of organisms or populations of interbreeding, living organisms that occupy one general geographic region and are essentially isolated reproductively from any other population of living organisms.

**How do creationists define the term *kind*?**

This term is also difficult to define, but certainly is not equivalent to the term *species* used by evolutionists. The term *kind* can be used generally for any easily recognized living form of animal or plant. Even evolutionists refer to organisms as belonging to some *kind*. The house cat *(Felis domestica)* and the lion *(Felis leo)* are placed in the same genus by modern taxonomists. Are these animals the same kind?

Much work needs to be done on delimiting the term *kind*. Very possibly the same methods of detecting interfertility, used by evolutionists in trying to delimit *species* could be used to arrive at some limits of kinds. Of course, no amount of research will identify the created kinds for the modern scientists.

## POSSIBLE MECHANISMS OF EVOLUTION

**What are the main categories of evidence that scientists use to support evolution?**

For ease of handling data and speed in covering the main categories I have developed the chart (on opposite page), which shows that the evolutionist scientists stress *similarities* that they find in these groups of data, whereas the creationist scientists emphasize *differences*.

**What about vestigial organs?**

*Vestigial* is a term that means nonfunctional. When evolu-

# A COMPARISON OF HOW EVOLUTIONISTS AND CREATIONISTS INTERPRET THE SAME SCIENTIFIC DATA

| Classes of Scientific Data | Summary of ways scientific data are used to support Uniform Evolution Model *EMPHASIZING SIMILARITIES* | Summary of ways scientific data are used to support Catastrophic Creation Model *EMPHASIZING DIFFERENCES* |
|---|---|---|
| Genetics and Variation | Imagined broad change: kind from kind, across kind. Differences due to recombinations and beneficial mutations that have accumulated; slow change. | Known limited change; only variation *within* kind. Mutations mostly harmful; no new traits; definite breeding gaps; *no connections between kinds.* |
| Classification | Similarities are basis of grouping due to supposed common gene pool of similar genes; supposed "history" of kinds. | Fixity of kinds; *no connections between distinct groups* caused by persistency of basic characteristics due to varieties from different beginnings. |
| Comparative Form or Anatomy | The degree of similarity is basis for degree of relationship; common gene pool, supposed common ancestry. | *No real connection of kinds;* similarities could be due to common plan by Creator God; consistency of master plan pressed. |
| Comparative Embryology | Similarity of structure is result of genetic relationship, supposed gene pool, supposed common ancestry. | *No real connection of kinds;* similarities could be due to common plan by Creator God; consistency of master plan pressed. |
| Geographic Distribution | Supposed descent with change due to modified environments. | Barriers and breeding resulted in centers of population growth; *no new kinds;* continental drift idea could be relevant. |
| Fossil Evidences | Presumably, successive layers provide evidence of succession of life forms; so-called actual history of related organism groups. | Definite gaps between kinds, *no intermediate forms;* no real geological column; worldwide flood possible cause; "living fossils" indicate fixity of kinds. |
| Dating Estimates | Data *interpreted* to mean long ages based on certain assumptions of constant decay rate, no contamination. Use radiometric and nonradiometric estimates plus geologic column. | Radiometric dating *assumptions are erroneous;* evidences of young earth noted; rapid burial likely; catastrophism. |

tionists consider certain organs or structures of living organisms for which they have no known function, they usually label them "vestigial." In horses certain bones are called vestigial metacarpels. About one hundred years ago, many organs in human beings, such as the thyroid glands, spleen, coccyx, and appendix, were labeled vestigial. Evolutionists have also interpreted vestigial organs as a "left over" from some previous stage of common ancestry of different organisms.

The appendix in human beings has been considered a "left over" from supposed ancestors who lived on a much more rough, tough food. Today biologists have identified the appendix as a part of the lymphatic system that cleanses the blood stream. Also, the functions of the thyroid and spleen are now known, and these organs are no longer labeled vestigial.

Careful studies of the human musculature prove that the coccyx is functional. Biologists now know that important muscles and tendons are attached to the coccyx; hence, an upright posture is more comfortable because of the coccyx.

## Does the entire system of evolutionist thinking rest upon one broad assumption?

Yes, because evolutionists have built their persuasively formulated position with great emphasis on similarities. When evolutionists see similarities between organisms they claim they have found a basis for relationship of those similar organisms. Since chimpanzees and human beings have similar skeletons, they must be related. Because embryos are similar, and blood and other proteins are similar, then all organisms that have such similarities must be related. So reason the evolutionists.

Thus this pattern of reasoning rests solely on the assumption that *the degree of relationship depends upon the degree of similarity*. Similarity, however, does not mean that any real familial relationship or lineage has been discovered. Evolutionists only assume relationships. Creation scientists can reasonably maintain that similarities are manifestations of the common plan of creation used by the Creator. Vertebrates all have similarity in the vertebral column and hence this can be used by human beings for classification purposes—all because God used a common plan in His creation of all vertebrates.

## What is the difference between microevolution and macroevolution?

The key to understanding these terms is found in the clear realization that evolutionists and creationists refer to two degrees of change of living things.

One degree of change involves changes such as those seen in the many varieties of dogs or in the many varieties of roses. Yet dogs produce only dogs and roses yield only roses. The degree of change is *within* easily recognizable kind: the dog-kind or the rose-kind. Some people use the term *microevolution* for this degree of change. The changes are small, or "micro-," but always *within* kind. Thus genetic variation within kind is all that is involved. The term *microevolution* could easily be discarded and the term *genetic variation* retained for this degree of change of living things.

The other degree of change involves changes that evolutionists claim occurred as the great variety of plants and animals came into existence through common ancestry. Somehow, birds and reptiles had common ancestry with fish. Supposedly, all multicellular animals had common ancestry with unicellular organisms, involving great changes. For example, winged creatures came from nonwinged forms, feathered creatures came from nonfeathered forms, and land animals came from aquatic animals. These are "macro-" changes that the evolutionist imagines but can in no way document from observed genetic patterns. No common ancestry is known or can be demonstrated by any controlled genetic breeding of animals or plants.

Hence genetic variation *within* kinds (which some unnecessarily call microevolution) is the only degree of change that is scientifically supported, but macroevolution is completely without observational foundation.

## How have evolutionists modified their favorite "theory"?

Initially evolution was called *Darwinism.* This was a term by which proponents referred to Charles Darwin's idea that new kinds of organisms came into existence as plants and animals competed. in their environment, and that natural selection occurred whereby the fitter forms survived and left the most offspring. This concept therefore includes variation plus natural selection.

Darwin, however, did not adequately explain the nature of, nor the source of, variation. When the thinking of Gregor Mendel was well understood in the early 1900s, evolution was referred to as *Neo-Darwinism,* a combination of Mendelian genetics and natural selection.

Evolutionists modified their position still further as biologists used mathematical means of analyzing biological population growth. Thus the modern synthetic "theory" is utilized today to refer to current combination of natural selection, Mendelian genetics, and mathematized population genetics.

### What is the mechanism for variation in living things?

As biological knowledge has increased, many reasons for variation in living things have been identified. All sexually reproducing organisms produce variable offspring in contrast to asexually reproducing organisms, which have offspring that essentially are carbon copies of the adult individuals.

Variation that results from the union of parts of two individuals is due to combinations and recombinations of chromosomes within cells, which in turn means multiple combinations and recombinations of genes. Further reasons for genetic variations are: chromosome parts can be interchanged, parts can be lost, or chromosomes can be unusually elongated by parts of other chromosomes. Most important is the fact that all genetic variations are *within* some recognizable kind.

## SIMILARITIES AND SIMPLICITY

### What is the difference between evolution and natural selection?

*Evolution* is the term used to refer to the grand scale changes of kinds through common ancestry, such as vertebrates from invertebrates, multicellular from unicellular, and life substance in cells from nonliving, inorganic matter. Evolution is the "molecules to man" thesis of great changes (also called macroevolution).

Many evolutionist scientists believe that macroevolution occurs through the process of *natural selection*. They believe that interaction of living organisms with their environment results in selection of those organisms most fitted for the environment. The fitted forms survive and reproduce progeny whereas the non-fitted are killed off.

*Natural survival* would be a better term than natural selection, since no selection really occurs as a result of any choice. Some individual organisms live, some do not. Hence, differential survival is what occurs, not natural selection.

**Has there been any evolution of the horse?**

There has been no evolution of the horse in the sense that a common ancestry of the horse and other organisms has been shown. Although evolutionists' ideas about the "evolution" of the horse vary, all reconstructions of skeletal materials have been considered representations of horses. Thus all that is involved is variation *within* some possible kind.

Worthy of note is the fact that horse skeleton samples are variable in size and have been collected over widely separated geographical regions. No sequence from one layer to another has been found in one geographic region, as seems so easily portrayed in textbooks authored by evolutionists.

Actually, horses are horses, and no macroevolution can be claimed; there is only variation *within* the horse-kind.

**Is the similarity of DNA\* materials a basis for relationship of kinds?**

Interestingly enough there is a striking similarity of DNA materials of different kinds according to current biochemical

---

\*These letters represent deoxyribonucleic acid. This material is found in the chromosomes of plants and animals and determines the appearance of physical traits.

studies. In fact, portions of DNA are interchangeable between kinds of organisms. Nevertheless, any claim of evolutionists that because of this, kinds of organisms have had common ancestry is once again an employment of the basic assumption: the degree of relationship depends on the degree of similarity. In no way is sheer similarity a means of establishing genetic or familial lineage between kinds.

**Why is the concept of creation and subsequent genetic variations within kinds a simpler explanation of origins than the concept of spontaneous generation of life and subsequent evolution through mutations (DNA errors)?**

To answer this question we should apply the law of parsimony to models about the origin of living things. According to the law of parsimony, the fewest number of factors are assumed in developing an explanation.

Often during a question-and-answer period evolutionists will claim that their position of assuming one spontaneous generation of life plus mutations is "simpler" than creation plus genetic variation within kinds. They like to point to all the creative acts needed to start all the created kinds that must have been on the earth at the beginning, and then contrast that with one supposed spontaneous generation of life.

In presenting this line of reasoning, however, evolutionists do not recognize that many, many mutations must be imagined for all the physical traits associated with the great variety of plants and animals, which supposedly had common ancestry with single cells. Mutations must be imagined, for example, for the appearance of shells, wings, legs, external skeletons (and then internal skeletons), scales (and then feathers), and on and on. So many traits are involved that no "simple," or parsimonious, situation is involved.

## LAWS OF THERMODYNAMICS

**What is the relationship of evolution and the first and second laws of thermodynamics?**

Evolution, that is, total evolutionism, violates both of these fundamental, well-established laws of science.

According to the first law of thermodynamics, nothing is now being created or destroyed. This is the principle of conservation of mass-energy—everything in the physical universe is being conserved.

According to the second law of thermodynamics, every system tends to move from order to disorder, available energy becomes less and less, until a state of complete randomness is reached. Thus all systems are "running down." This is known as entropy.

According to total evolutionism, there has been an increasing order of things through time as the universe, including the earth, supposedly evolved from eternal matter. Life arose, and highly ordered man came from a long common ancestry with the amoeba (megaevolution is "molecules to man" or "amoeba to man" in different textbooks). Hence evolutionists invoke some universal law of innovation and integration, which has *not* been identified at all. The evolutionists' imagined integration of molecules into planets and later into living substance, and finally into humankind, is in complete violation of the first and second laws of thermodynamics. (Note that the universe would have had a beginning, a time when it was wound up, yet according to the first law there can only be conservation of what is. Only a Creator could have started what now is being conserved.)

Actually, solid scientific data are accumulating that clearly substantiate that principles of conservation and disintegration are the universal conditions that prevail in the universe. All reproductive processes are essentially conservation processes whereby the life that is on the earth is conserved. Yet the sun energy is becoming less and less, mutations are evidence of disorder, and all living things die. The real conditions on earth and in the universe, as far as they are known, fit the first and second laws, but do not fit any supposed universal law of innovation and integration.

Note: Total evolution also is in complete disagreement with a basic law of biology, the law of biogenesis, or the concept that life comes from life. Since total evolution is based on the concept of spontaneous generation of life from inorganic matter, then there is a patent violation of the law of biogenesis.

**If all systems move toward disorder when left unattended, how can evolutionists account for life "evolving" out of so-called simple orders?**

Plainly and simply put, they cannot. This is the basic gap underlying their whole system of thought. Evolutionists cannot show how cells came into existence, though they point to so-called synthetic cells or proteinoids that have been produced in their laboratories. These are not real cells.

# 3

# What About Dating Methods?

## OLD VERSUS YOUNG EARTH

**How old is the earth?**

The most direct and unqualified answer is that no one knows. For centuries human beings have been estimating both the age of the earth and the age of the universe. But even in the scientific era there are no compelling, scientific measurements of the age of either the earth or the universe.

Scientists have used various means to try to *estimate* the age of the earth by calculating various rates of change (such as cooling of the earth, sedimentation, accumulation of salt concentrations in the ocean, and, more recently, radioactive or radiometric decay and fission tracks). All of these methods involve problems, as will be pointed out in answers to other questions in this chapter.

**Are there any evidences of a young earth?**

Definitely. Some of the evidences, however, involve complicated arguments and reasons.

One easily grasped idea is that there are not large enough concentrations of salts of various elements in the oceans* for the earth to be as old as evolutionists claim it is.

---

*These conditions are discussed at length by Harold Camping in his article, "Let the Oceans Speak" in *Creation Research Society Quarterly*, January 1974, (1) pp. 39-45.

Any "clock" or chronometer of the age of the earth involves assumptions that are not testable. A fundamental difficulty is that no one knows the initial conditions of the earth, so no "zero setting" can ever be determined for any "clock."

## Is the magnetic field of the earth decaying?

A complicated set of ideas about the magnetic field of the earth is discussed by Dr. Thomas G. Barnes in a special monograph titled, "Origin and Destiny of the Earth's Magnetic Field" (San Diego: Institute for Creation Research, 1973). Dr. Barnes concluded from his calculations that the origin of the magnetic field of the earth was much less than twenty thousand years ago. He based his work on precise data that has been collected for over one hundred years.

One might react at first with a "so-what" response. The magnetic field, however, deflects cosmic radiation from the surface of the earth. This may have a great deal to do with the health of human beings. But the decay rate of the magnetic field is slow enough that scientists now predict that the magnetic field will not disappear until sometime between A.D. 3900 and 11,000. This, of course, assumes that the decay rate will remain about the same as that derived from data available today.

## What is the basis for the evolutionists' claim of an old earth?

Frankly, the basis is found in their own ideas. To account for even the remotest possibility of the changes they imagine, evolutionists must postulate immense lengths of time. Although they have long held the idea of an old earth and an old universe, they have tried in recent decades to find evidence to support their preconceived ideas.

Evolutionists first tried to support this notion of immense lengths of time by developing the geologic column, which is only a deduced assemblage of rocks. As further explained in chapter 4, the geologic column does not exist anywhere on the surface of the earth.

# RADIOACTIVE DATING METHODS

## What is the carbon-14 dating process?

This is a method for estimating the "age" of organic material. The process involves formation of carbon-14 in the atmosphere due to a complex set of reactions between cosmic radiation from outer space and atmospheric nitrogen-14. During the process nitrogen is changed into carbon-14. Carbon-14 is usually assumed to be in equilibrium with "natural" carbon, which is carbon-12. All carbon unites with oxygen to form carbon dioxide, and carbon dioxide is utilized in green plants during the glucose-making process of photosynthesis. Thus both radioactive carbon and nonradioactive carbon can be found in plant tissue. By determining the ratio of carbon-14 to carbon-12 it is possible to calculate the "age" of plant materials. It is possible in turn to calculate the "age" of animals that have taken in carbon-14 through the plant material consumed.

## What is the uranium-lead dating process?

This is another means of estimating "ages" of rocks of the earth's surface. The uranium-lead method is a complex of three decay chains of uranium and thorium into lead and helium, with a check phase involving "common" lead, which is not a product of radioactive decay. Basically, a ratio of uranium to lead is determined for a rock sample (an igneous rock) and then the "age" of the rock sample can be calculated.

## What is the potassium-argon dating process?

This is yet another method for estimating "ages" of igneous rocks of the earth's surface. This method involves changes whereby potassium-40 decays by the "electron-capture" process into argon-40. This method is usually calibrated, or compared, to the uranium-lead method.

# LIMITATIONS OF RADIOACTIVE DATING METHODS

## What are limitations of the carbon–14 dating process?

The carbon-14 dating method can only be applied to materials containing carbon. Thus it cannot be used in estimating the age of sedimentary layers to indicate the age of the earth.

Dr. Willard Libby, originator of the carbon-14 dating method, has stated that his confidence in the method for determining "ages" for the past six thousand years is based on the fact that "ages" derived by the carbon-14 method can be checked against the records of humankind. He has stated that he would be confident in extending the method to gain dates up to ten thousand years ago, but beyond that the sample becomes smaller and the margin of error increases greatly.

Further, scientists have determined that carbon-14 and carbon-12 are not in an equilibrium as those who use the method have assumed. The rate of formation and the rate of decay of carbon-14 differ by at least 24 percent. Also, the ratio of decay of carbon-14 may not have been constant if the atmosphere was different in the past; likewise the amount of "natural" carbon in the atmosphere might have varied in the distant past.

All in all, the use of the carbon-14 dating method is restricted to the degree that results can be checked against the records of human beings.

### What are limitations of other radioactive dating methods?

Each method involves the assumption that the rate of decay has been constant. There is no way to know how valid this assumption is over the immense lengths of time imagined by evolutionists and estimated by these methods. Each method involves the assumption that no decay elements (no lead or argon) were present at the beginning of the earth. Yet, nearly all lead in rocks or minerals might be considered primordial. Then the uranium-lead calculations would be thrown way off. There are strong possibilities for contamination by atmospheric argon, and a correction factor must be used. Specifically, no one knows the initial or primeval ratios of elements. More technical limitations are listed by Dr. Henry Morris in *Scientific Creationism*. (The method involving decay of rubidium 87 into strontium 87 is considered so unreliable that it has been discarded.)

## Do scientists gain any absolute times with their radioactive dating methods?

No, because the only objective facts gained from radioactive dating methods are ratios of certain elements found in rocks today—on the surface of the earth or even on the surface of the moon. But again, no one knows the initial or primeval ratio of elements. Radioactive dating methods, based upon certain assumptions that are open to serious challenge today, can be used only to gain estimates of ages of rocks.

## Is the amount of time imagined by evolutionists long enough for the slow processes that they believe caused the present conditions and life forms?

One of the favorite responses of evolutionists to comments or criticisms of evolutionary thinking by creationist scientists is, "Well, given enough time the changes we are talking about are possible."

How realistic is their position? Not realistic at all. In the first place, the greater the span of time imagined, the greater the opportunity for decay and degeneration of any possible new form. Also, researchers have shown mathematically that not even enough time has been imagined by evolutionists for the changes from single cells to complex multi-cellular organisms like human beings.

Another fact is that time alone cannot supply the necessary requirements for living organisms, such as: (1) an open system, (2) an adequate energy supply, (3) energy conversion systems, and (4) a control system. Just the very existence of the solar system could be a source of the first two requirements, but living things require all four of the above. Only a Supreme Intelligence can be the cause or source of *all* these requirements.

## GENESIS DAYS AND GAP "THEORY"

### How long were the days of Genesis during the creation week?

Lengthy papers and large sections of books have been written in attempts to answer this question. I find it most logical to accept the twenty-four-hour, night-day cycle as the ancient Hebrews (and some Jews today) considered the "evening and morning" phrase in Genesis 1.

I remind those who refer to II Peter 3:8 that the phrase "one day is with the Lord as a thousand years, and a thousand years as one day" does *not* mean that the day of the Lord is equal to a thousand years. For me, any effort to lengthen the night-day cycle of creation beyond a natural length of twenty-four hours involves several problems:

1. If I assume a normal photosynthetic (food-making) process in plant life of the third day, how could that process occur if there was no radiant energy from the sun (that major light in the sky was assigned a day later)?

2. How could normal pollination of fruit trees of the third day occur by insects (there possibly being no winds in the Garden of Eden) if those winged forms were not created or made until two days later?

We read in Exodus 20:11, "For in six days the LORD made heaven and earth, the sea, and all that in them is," and again in Exodus 31:17 "for in six days the LORD made heaven and earth." Therefore, my belief that the universe and the earth were created by the Word of God is the basis for accepting the twenty-four-hour length of each day in the creation week. To me this is fully consistent with the Word of God.

## How does Exodus 20:11 relate to the gap "theory"?

To my mind, there is no real basis for any gap "theory." Though the Hebrew can be translated so that some break in God's actions may have occurred after Genesis 1:1, there is clearly no basis for millions of years according to those who have studied ancient Targums and other writings of Hebrew scholars. God "made heaven and earth, the sea, and all that in them is." That this encompasses Genesis 1:1 through Genesis 1:31 inclusively seems most logical to me.

# 4

## What About Changes of the Earth's Surface?

### GEOLOGIC COLUMN AND THE GENESIS FLOOD

**What is the significance of the geologic column?**

The geologic column is primarily significant to the evolutionist geologist and the evolutionist biologist. It was the main basis for estimating time until the development of radioactive or radiometric dating methods. There is still a strong tendency to compare all calculated "ages" from radiometric methods with estimated "ages" of rocks. I say estimated "ages" of rocks since the geologic column has been used world-wide as a type of yardstick of time. Although not an independent measure of time, this imagined "sequence" of rocks is the basis for ordering presumed evolutionary changes of living things from least complex to most complex. Basically, the "age" of a rock layer is assigned according to fossils found in the rocks; and, in turn, the "age" of a fossil is assigned according to the rock layer in which it is found.

**Does the complete geologic column exist anywhere on the earth's surface?**

The geologic column is totally man-made as far as sequence from the "oldest" fossil–containing Cambrian—to the most recent and uppermost Cenozoic layers. At no place on the surface of the earth can all of the layers of the geologic column be found. True, there are many exposed "local" columns from which the one main geologic column has been "built." Based on studies of

# GEOLOGICAL COLUMN, SCALE OF TIME, AND PRESUMED EVOLUTION OF LIVING FORMS

| PERIOD | EPOCH | TIME (millions of years ago) | BIOTIC DEVELOPMENT |
|---|---|---|---|
| **CENOZOIC ERA** | | | |
| Quaternary | Helocene Pleistocene | 1 | Placental mammals, including man, dominate scene; many species of plants and animals became extinct. |
| Tertiary | Pliocene Miocene Oligocene Eocene Paleocene | 70 | Early man; mammals became dominant; forests were widespread. |
| **MESOZOIC ERA** | | | |
| Cretaceous | (periods divided into upper and lower to designate epochs) | 135 | Dinosaurs thrived and later became extinct; gymnosperms declined. |
| Jurassic | | 180 | Marsupial mammals increased; angiosperms rose from gymnosperms. |
| Triassic | | 225 | Some dinosaurs, birds and egg-laying mammals; gymnosperms were dominant plants. |
| **PALEOZOIC ERA** | | | |
| Permian | | 270 | Mammal-like reptiles appeared; dominant fernlike plants decreased. |
| Pennsylvanian (Carboniferous) | | 330 | Reptiles rose; great forests of fernlike plants and gymnosperms. |
| Mississippian (Carboniferous) | (periods divided into upper and lower to designate epochs) | 350 | Amphibians rose; first vascular plants; fishes become widespread. |
| Devonian | | 400 | Insects rose; species of fish became very numerous; algae were dominant plants. |
| Silurian | | 440 | Fishes appeared; many species of invertebrates developed; some land plants. |
| Ordovician | | 500 | First primitive vertebrates and protochordates; algae were widespread. |
| Cambrian | | 600 | |
| **PROTEROZOIC ERA (Precambrian)** | | | |
| Keweenawan | | 1,700 | Some algae, fungi, and modern invertebrates; fossil record questionable. |
| Huronian | | | |
| **ARCHEOZOIC ERA (Precambrian)** | | | |
| No known basis for systematic division. | | 2,600 | No fossil record; it is assumed that the first living forms began less than 3 billion years ago. |
| **AZOIC ERA** | | | |
| | | 4,500 | Waterless; oldest rock on the earth estimated to be 3.4 billion years old. |
| **COSMIC ERA** | | | |

A typical timetable of the theoretical geological ages. Nowhere on the surface of the earth does one find all these layers present. The geological column is only hypothesized by historical geologists, based upon correlating rocks from many different places.

many local columns, geologists have deduced what they *think* was one logical sequence of deposition of sediments, one on top of another (although some layers are completely missing in a representative local column like the Grand Canyon).

## What is the significance of abrupt changes of life forms found in the fossil record?

The abrupt changes of life forms fully evident in the fossil record has long been a serious problem for scientists. Clearly the fact of abrupt changes is a basis for interpreting that major changes of the earth's surface have occurred in the past. Of course, such theoretical changes are unrepeatable and no check of any interpretation is possible. Most evolutionist geologists explain the abrupt changes in fossil assemblages by major land mass changes which occurred. Creationist geologists, however, interpret the most abrupt changes as changes associated with the world-wide flood of Noah. They believe that at the time of the great flood, organisms were living in certain water habitats, semi-land habitats, or land habitats, and thus were buried at different levels according to their habitat. Those in the water were destroyed first; those in semi-land habitats, later; and those in land habitats, last.

## How do creationists explain the increasing complexity of life in the rock strata at the Grand Canyon?

Since organisms live in different habitats (or ecological niches) today, it is reasonable to conclude that a similar distribution of life forms existed in the past. Thus creationist geologists explain the pattern of increasing complexity illustrated in fossils in different layers at different depths in the Grand Canyon as correlating with presumed habitat distribution in the past and differential burial. There are problems. Marine and land fossil forms are found in rather closely alternating layers. Could these conditions be associated with the probable immensely cataclysmic and catastrophic nature of the Noachian Flood? Creationist geologists think so, but they acknowledge that a fully naturalistic explanation for what appropriately is conceived as supernatural is impossible.

## What about circular reasoning with regard to the geologic column?

The charge of "circular reasoning" about evolutionary consideration of the artificially produced geologic column is commonly heard from creationist scientists. Evolutionist geologists assign "ages" to particular rock layers according to the fossil evidence contained in them. They reason that since living forms on the earth have changed from least complex to most complex, they must assign an "age" to rock layers with fossils found in them in keeping with the accepted evolutionary sequence of living things. Evolutionary (molecules to man) thinking is the basis for development of the artificial geologic column, but then this geologic column is used as a basis of "supporting" supposed evolutionary changes.

## What is the significance of widely distributed sedimentary rocks?

Most geologists believe that all sedimentary rocks (sandstone, limestone, and conglomerate) were formed by slow accumulation of rock fragments and sediments of other rocks under water and that rivers and other running water transported rock fragments and sediments to oceans and other collection basins.

Today, expansive amounts of sedimentary rocks are exposed or lie near the earth's surface in all land masses. Huge extents of sedimentary rocks are evident in Siberia, Europe, Africa, North and South America, and Australia. Thus at some time or another water has covered major portions of the earth's surface. Evolutionist geologists will only admit to multiple *local* flooding in the past. Creationist geologists, however, conclude that such world-wide distribution of sedimentary rocks is an excellent basis for the world-wide flooding and rapid sedimentation associated with the Noachian Flood.

## CHANGING ENVIRONMENTS AND
## UNIFORMITARIANISM

### Do changes in the natural environment result in changes of living things?

Volcanoes, earthquakes, torrential rainfall and water runoff, and other catastrophic changes have direct bearing on living organisms in any affected region. Mass destruction of fish, complete burn off of plant life, and other gross alterations of habitats of living organisms on the surface of the earth are repeatedly documented.

However, all the gross changes in specific regions during centuries of observation (both casual and meticulously planned) support the conclusion that *no new kinds* of organisms have resulted from environmental changes. Such findings directly contradict evolutionists' suppositions that new kinds of living organisms have come into existence as survivors of environmental changes.

### How long have living things existed on the earth?

This question is related to the question, How old is the earth? Just as no person can give a scientifically conclusive answer regarding the "age" of the earth, no one can scientifically determine how long life has existed on the earth.

### What is uniformitarianism? Is the "present the key to the past"?

The term *uniformitarianism* is used to represent the thinking of most geologists that today's forces or causes of change have generally been operative in past ages. Often this thesis has been characteristically stated as "the present is the key to the past."

Uniformitarianism should not be confused with the term *uniformity*. All reasoning men and women accept and fully utilize the concept of uniformity, that is, the idea that natural events and causes are regular and repetitive. Scientists assume a basic uniformity of events in the natural environment. Such conditions are basic to the formulation of scientific ("natural") laws.

47

Supporters of uniformitarianism regularly talk about events in the past of greater dimension and scope than anything known during the life of any investigator. Observers never see mountain building (except some volcanic mountains), continental glaciation, or complete erosion of mountain ranges in the degree of change imagined by uniformitarian "historical" geologists. Actually, *the present is a key to the present only*. No part of reality can be associated with the concept of uniformitarianism; whereas real, actual events are regularly shown to be examples of ongoing *uniformity* of the natural environment.

## ICE AGES

**What are some of the evidences geologists use to support their idea that masses of ice covered large portions of North America?**

Throughout northern portions of New York, Pennsylvania, Ohio, Indiana, Illinois, and most of Wisconsin and Minnesota there are many hills, ridges, and lake regions. The most logical interpretation of the formation of such land features is glacial action from a source in northern Canada over this broad geographic region. There is a wide range of names used, such as moraines (lateral and terminal), eskers, and drumlins. Very possibly rock debris was pushed south across many square miles by huge masses of ice. Also running melt water under the ice and from the southernmost edge may have been a significant transport agent of ground, even pulverized, rock materials produced by moving ice.

**How many ice ages were there?**

According to majority consensus there were four different advances of ice over much of North America. Of course it is impossible to check such an interpretation since there is no possibility of repeating the events. The arrangement of ridges and hills attributed to glacial action is basic to this interpretation. A minority of geologists have proposed that actually there was only one huge ice mass covering portions of North America in the past, but that there were two, three, or possibly four different "outlines" of the southern edge due to differential melting as climatic changes occurred.

## FOSSILIZATION AND "WRONG ORDER" FOSSILS

### What are fossils and how are they formed?

Fossils are preserved hard parts; impressions, casts or molds of parts; or mineralized remains of previous living organisms.

No one has seen how a fossil was formed. The process presumably involved such rapid coverage of an organism that processes of decay and disintegration due to oxidation and/or bacterial decomposition were prevented. Although volcanic ash apparently covered some organisms, most fossils are found in sedimentary rocks. These rocks were supposedly formed after accumulation of rock fragments under water. Creationist scientists therefore maintain that fossils could be evidence of organisms destroyed in the Noachian Flood.

Presumably compaction and cementation processes that were probably involved in formation of sedimentary rocks resulted in pressure exerted upon animal and plant parts. Often small specimens are completely carbonized, that is, composed of residual carbon. Also fossils were formed due to replacement of plant tissues by chemicals and minerals. This is the accepted explanation for petrified wood found in Yellowstone National Park and in the Petrified National Forest.

### What is petrified wood?

Petrified wood is an example of fossil material that has supposedly formed by the replacement of plant tissues with chemicals and minerals. This is a logical explanation. Fossil wood, as this material might be called, is very hard, dense, and hence quite heavy. The rate at which replacement of plant tissue occurred is not known, but most probably the necessary processes occurred while the tree material was underground and in an area where much underground movement of chemicals and minerals occurred repeatedly and through a significant length of time.

## What are polystrate tree trunks?

Polystrate tree trunks are fossilized trees ranging in length from a few feet to about 55 feet. They are completely surrounded by accumulated rock fragments and sediments that evidently hardened into sedimentary layers. Commonly found in quarries, the tree trunks are oriented vertically, horizontally, or at a variety of slant positions.

How polystrate tree trunks were forced into this variety of positions is a significant problem to geologists. Evolutionist geologists are willing to suggest sudden burial due to rapid sedimentation because of some local flood. Since creationist geologists emphasize the wide distribution of polystrate tree trunks in areas on both the European and North American continents, they utilize these fossil materials as circumstantial evidence for the world-wide Noachian Flood reported in Genesis, based on the actual report of human participants.

## How are coal and oil explained according to the evolution model? . . . according to the creation model?

Evolutionist geologists have long maintained that the formation of coal and oil required immense periods of time. Presumably masses of plant and vegetative materials were buried under rock fragments and sediments that accumulated under water. Then, presumably due to compaction and pressure, the plant and vegetable material very slowly was converted to coal in Pennsylvania, West Virginia, Ohio, and regions in Europe and Asia (or converted to oil in Texas, California, and regions east and southeast of the Mediterranean Sea).

In recent years industrial plant experimenters have successfully produced both coal and oil in their laboratories. Such coal and oil have been expensive to produce but are of excellent high energy potential. Therefore creationist scientists are now maintaining that coal and oil may have been formed in a relatively short time.

## Is it true that fossils have been found "out of place" in the fossil record?

There are multiple reports of pollen and other parts of flowering plants in the lowest layers of the geologic column. In fact, reports show that most of the major kinds of plants and animals have been found throughout the rock layers that comprise the geologic column. These findings are summarized in the charts on the following page. The length of the vertical lines represents the existence of kinds of plants and animals throughout supposed geologic time. A conclusive generalization drawn from these charts is that each major form or kind of plant and animal is shown to have a separate and distinct history from all other forms or kinds. All this information can be used to support the concept of fixity of kinds as the present-day equivalent to the Biblical phrases, "after his kind" and "after their kind."

## Is the fossil bird *Archaeopteryx* a missing link?

*Archaeopteryx* does not qualify as a "missing link" or transitional form. Many scientists, however, consider the *Archaeopteryx* as a bird with reptilian characteristics, or, as some scientists would state the relationship, a reptile with some bird characteristics. Presence of evidence of wing structures plus other minor features are facts that ornithologists, scientists who specialize in the study of birds, use to label *Archaeopteryx* a bird. Of course no one knows whether such a bird ever flew. In fact, some scientists are now reasoning that the animal only ran, as an ostrich which is primarily a running bird and flies very little.

## How do you explain the absence of intermediate forms in the fossil record?

This absence is best explained by the excellent likelihood that no intermediate or transitional forms have ever existed. Just as there is no conclusive evidence from animal breeding or plant breeding records of the existence of fully fertile transitions or hybrids between major kinds of organisms, the same general condition exists as far as the fossil record is concerned. The

# GENERALIZED GEOLOGICAL RECORD FOR PLANTS

| PERIOD | Fungi | Algae | Mosses | Hepaticae | Psilophytales | Equisitinae (Horsetails) | Lycopodales (Club-mosses) | Filicales (Ferns) | Pteridospermae | Cycadales | Benettitales | Ginkgoales | Cordiates | Coniferales | Monocotyledones | Dicotyledones |
|---|---|---|---|---|---|---|---|---|---|---|---|---|---|---|---|---|
| Present | | | | | | | | | | | | | | | | |
| Pliocene | | | | | | | | | | | | | | | | |
| Miocene | | | | | | | | | | | | | | | | |
| Oligocene | | | | | | | | | | | | | | | | |
| Eocene | | | | | | | | | | | | | | | | |
| Paleocene | | | | | | | | | | | | | | | | |
| Cretaceous | | | | | | | | | | | | | | | | |
| Jurassic | | | | | | | | | | | | | | | | |
| Triassic | | | | | | | | | | | | | | | | |
| Permian | | | | | | | | | | | | | | | | |
| Carboni- ferous | | | | | | | | | | | | | | | | |
| Devonian | | | | | | | | | | | | | | | | |
| Silurian | | | | | | | | | | | | | | | | |
| Ordovician | | | | | | | | | | | | | | | | |
| Cambrian | | | | | | | | | | | | | | | | |

Generalized geological record of plants is shown here. Solid vertical lines represent duration of existence of each plant group. Broken line portions indicate some doubt as to the earliest appearance of some groups. No common ancestors are known.

# GENERALIZED GEOLOGICAL RECORD FOR ANIMALS

| PERIOD | Radiolaria | Foraminifera | Spongiae | Hydrozoa | Cystoidea | Blastoidea | Crinoidea | Echinoidea | Brachiopoda | Gastropoda | Insecta | Crustacea | Arachnida | Pisces | Amphibia | Reptilia | Mammalia | Aves |
|---|---|---|---|---|---|---|---|---|---|---|---|---|---|---|---|---|---|---|
| Present | | | | | | | | | | | | | | | | | | |
| Pliocene | | | | | | | | | | | | | | | | | | |
| Miocene | | | | | | | | | | | | | | | | | | |
| Oligocene | | | | | | | | | | | | | | | | | | |
| Eocene | | | | | | | | | | | | | | | | | | |
| Paleocene | | | | | | | | | | | | | | | | | | |
| Cretaceous | | | | | | | | | | | | | | | | | | |
| Jurassic | | | | | | | | | | | | | | | | | | |
| Triassic | | | | | | | | | | | | | | | | | | |
| Permian | | | | | | | | | | | | | | | | | | |
| Carboni- ferous | | | | | | | | | | | | | | | | | | |
| Devonian | | | | | | | | | | | | | | | | | | |
| Silurian | | | | | | | | | | | | | | | | | | |
| Ordovician | | | | | | | | | | | | | | | | | | |
| Cambrian | | | | | | | | | | | | | | | | | | |

Generalized geological record of animals is portrayed in this chart. Vertical lines represent duration of existence in each animal group. No common ancestors are known.

conclusion can be stated over and over that kinds of plants and kinds of animals are distinct.

Some evolutionist scientists say that the absence of intermediate forms is possibly due to the absence of conditions conducive to fossilization when these supposed intermediate forms existed. Such an interpretation is an idea proposed to meet the particular situation, that is, an ad hoc concept offered to explain away the difficult fact of the absence of intermediate forms. No test or check of such an idea is possible, so no real explanation is presented.

**Would you consider *Archaeopteryx* and *Seymouria* as transitional forms between "kinds"?**

These are not true transitional forms. They are merely examples of fossil forms that show some characteristics of more than one possible kind. *Archaeopteryx* had features that are interpreted as similar to reptiles and birds. *Seymouria* had features that are interpreted as similar to amphibians and reptiles.

On the basis of such similarities to different possible kinds of organisms, evolutionists insist that these forms were transitional forms. Yet no genetic relationship could ever be established, and therefore no familial lineage or relationship can truly be documented. *Archaeopteryx* and *Seymouria* can logically be considered as previous living organisms that had characteristics similar to several kinds of organisms, just as the platypus has characteristics similar to beavers, hairy mammals, and egg-laying animals.

**Do you think "transitional forms" will ever be found in the fossil records?**

Naturally a person should be careful about declaring what will be found in rock layers. Charles Darwin once expressed great hope that fossils he considered missing from sedimentary rocks would be located. He expected other scientists to "fill in" the record, and hence support his ideas about gradual changes among organisms over a long time span. After more than one hundred years the same basic gaps in the fossil record still exist.

I do not expect transitional forms to be found, because I sincerely doubt that any transitional forms between basic kinds have ever existed.

## What are "living fossils"?

"Living fossils" is a label for plants and animals that were supposed to have been extinct for at least several millions of years, but which have been found alive and thriving on earth. The very existence of "living fossils" is evidence for fixity of kinds. Just a few examples of such organisms are listed on the opposite page with references to the adopted geologic time scale..

## OVERTHRUSTS AND CONTINENTAL DRIFT

### Is it true that some "old" layers of rocks are located over "younger" rock layers?

Conditions of this type are known in various parts of the world. One of the most famous examples is Chief Mountain in Glacier Park, Montana, just south of the Canadian border. In this example rocks labeled pre-Cambrian are over rocks marked as Cretaceous. Chief Mountain is a part of what some geologists call the Lewis Overthrust. Creationist geologists, however, maintain that there is no real evidence of an overthrust.

Many smaller and more limited examples with rocks "out of order" can be found with "real" evidence for lateral movement of rock layers over each other that resulted in an overthrust.

### What is the "real" evidence of overthrusts of rock layers?

Usually the evidence cited for an actual overthrust of rock layers includes the presence of brecciation (ground-up rock particles), gouging, and slickensides as mechanical features of rock movement. In a good example of an overthrust area in the Santa Rita Mountains in Arizona, a gouge layer about three feet thick composed of ground-up rock powder was identified. This has been accepted as clear evidence that one block of rock has moved against another block of rock. Similarly, in the Tortolita Mountains in Arizona a layer of breccia—fifteen to twenty feet

# "LIVING FOSSILS"

| | | |
|---|---|---|
| 1. | Crinoids: | Flowerlike echinoderms, commonly called sea lilies or feather stars. There are about 2,100 species of fossil crinoids and about 800 species of living representatives. Found in Paleozoic strata. |
| 2. | Lingula: | Within the phylum Brachiopoda, the genus *Lingula*, which currently lives in the oceans of the world, is found attached to the bottom in mud or sand by a peduncle. This same genus is found in the fossil marine fauna of the Cambrian. |
| 3. | Tuatara: | This relic of the past is the only survivor of the order Rhynchocephalia, or beak-headed reptiles. Living specimens have been found only on islands off New Zealand, where they live in holes on sandy hills by the shore. The skeleton of one of these reptiles found in Jurassic deposits of Europe is almost exactly like the living tuatara. Fossil evidence of this organism is found in the Early Cretaceous, which supposedly leaves a time gap of 135 million years. |
| 4. | Coelacanth: | In 1937 a coelacanth was caught alive east of London, Cape Province, South Africa. According to the paleontological record the last coelacanth lived approximately 70 million years ago. More specimens have been taken near Madagascar and the South Africa vicinity. "The bony structures of our modern Coelacanths are almost exactly the same as those left by Coelacanths hundreds of millions of years ago." (Smith, J. L. B. *The Search Beneath the Sea*. Henry Holt and Co., New York, 1956) |
| 5. | Neopilina: | On May 6, 1952, ten specimens of this deep-sea mollusk were dredged from a depth of 3,590 meters off the Mexican Coast. According to paleontologists *Neopilina* became extinct about 280 million years ago during the Devonian period. It is not found in intervening rocks. |
| 6. | Cycads: | *Zamia* grows in parts of Florida, the West Indies, and South America. The East Indian genus *Cycas* attains a height of 67 feet and is 40 inches in diameter. Fossil cycads, quite abundant in Mesozoic formations, have been found in many areas with abundant remains in the Black Hills. |
| 7. | Metasequoia: | Fossils of *Metasequoia* make it the most abundant genus of the Taxodiaceae, or cypresslike family, in North America in the Upper Cretaceous to Miocene formations. Ever since 1946 many living specimens of *Metasequoia* have been found in China. (Chaney, Ralph W. "A Revision of Fossil *Sequoia* and *Taxodium* in Western North America Based on the Recent Discovery of Metasequoia," *Transactions of American Philosophical Society*, 40 (3): 171-263, 1951). |

thick—was identified. There was also evidence of marked fluting or slickensides much like the striae or scratches caused by glaciers.

## How could fossil marine forms come to be at the top of some mountains?

There are examples of such a condition in North America and Europe. The "answer" agreed upon is that massive rock uplift has occurred resulting in elevation of rock materials that accumulated under water at one time. Marine life forms were covered and fossilization occurred. No one can possibly explain for sure what forces were involved in such supposed massive rock uplifts.

## What is continental drift and what are the possible mechanisms for it?

Twenty years ago most geologists thought of the continents as fixed or stationary. At that time only a small number of scientists promoted the idea that the major continents had broken apart from some common land mass. Thus the idea that the continents might have fitted together at one time to form a single continent is an old one. Today this idea has become very popular and the idea of drifting continents is called *plate tectonics* (a term for deformation of the earth's crust).

The supposed mechanics for continental drifting are (1) sea floor spreading where two plates (land masses) move apart with new material from a deeper portion of the earth's crust being added between the plates to form new oceanic crust, as at the Mid-Atlantic Ridge; (2) horizontal slippage of one rock mass past another, as along the San Andreas fault in California; and (3) convergence of two plates as one overthrusts another producing supposed deformation, as at the Peru-Chile Trench and the Andes Mountains of South America associated with it.

Since there are no known slow-acting causes or forces that can explain these three mechanisms, creationist geologists maintain that such changes were accomplished by rapid processes that do not occur today, such as might have been accomplished in the Noachian Flood.

## CHANGING COMPLEXITY OF LIFE ON EARTH

**If evolutionists were correct wouldn't that mean that the variety of life forms should have increased during so-called geologic time?**

If new species and kinds of organisms have been appearing on earth as evolutionists want people to believe, then a reasonable conclusion would be that the variety of life forms should have increased. Contrary to that expectation there is much evidence to support the argument that there has been a loss or reduction of plant and animal variety. Many forms have become extinct, like the dinosaur, sabre-toothed tiger, mammoth, Irish elk, great ferns, and so forth. Instead of increase, it is more reasonable to refer to loss and extinction of many plant and animal kinds and species. Even today there is much concern over the lengthening list of endangered species.

**How did Noah fit all the animals into the Ark? Did he include fishes? birds?**

This is a complex question. It must be answered in terms of kinds of animals and not broadened to include all the multiple species and varieties that are known today. One biologist has estimated that only two thousand different kinds of animals were included on the Ark.

Evidently God directed the animals to come to the Ark. Representatives of all the major kinds were taken aboard, including all birds, all land-dwelling reptiles and mammals, and possibly some terrestrial amphibians. No water-dwelling groups were included as no instructions were given for them.

**What about the problem of food supply and waste removal for the animals on the Ark?**

Both problems of food supply and waste removal might have been greatly reduced if God caused some kind of extended or intermittent hibernation or slowdown of bodily functions of the animals in the Ark. As to the care of the animals on the Ark, there is good reason to believe that God supernaturally controlled events. The biblical report is consistently supernatural.

# 5

# Where Did the Universe Come From?

## "THEORIES" ON ORIGIN OF UNIVERSE AND SOLAR SYSTEM

### What are some of the "theories" about the origin of the universe?

For centuries human beings have been making guesses about the origin of the universe. Customarily the "guesser" imagines some amount of undifferentiated matter, uses known laws of nature, and assumes almost infinite time in formulating an idea. Unfortunately, the naturalist usually rules out any intervention by a divine Creator. He ignores the first cause of all things, leaving the only other position of the eternal existence of matter, which in some unaided manner gave rise to the universe.

Though many different variations might be mentioned, the two favorite explanations for the origin of the universe have been (1) the big bang "theory," and (2) the steady state "theory" (sometimes referred to as continuous creation).

According to the popularly accepted big bang "theory" some existing dense material or particle exploded, from which came helium and eventually the other elements, stars, suns, planets, and comets. Based on the way astronomers interpret light coming from distant objects to the earth (this concerns the concept of "red shift" of stellar light), the present universe is supposedly still expanding.

The steady state "theory" involves the idea of an infinitely old and large universe that is constantly expanding. Somehow new matter was supposed to appear out of nowhere to replenish matter lost in any given region of the universe. If the amount of matter contained in the universe remained the same then a steady-state situation would prevail. This idea has been almost completely discarded.

## What are some of the "theories" about the origin of the solar system?

Many proposals have been put forth since the mid-1600s. The longest lasting, though repeatedly modified, has been the nebular "hypothesis," which involved the idea that the solar system came from a disc-shaped gas cloud. Then there was the collision "hypothesis" that a passing comet tore a quantity of material from the sun, and that this material cooled and formed the earth and other planets. Then the planetismal "hypothesis" was offered in place of the nebular approach; the solar system was thought to have formed by an accumulation of small solid particles that revolved around a central mass. These ideas have been followed by another nebular "hypothesis," a dust cloud "hypothesis," and a protoplanet "hypothesis."

No evolutionary scheme on the origin of the earth's solar system, once adequately examined, has survived long. Since they will not accept the unchanging answers contained in Genesis 1, naturalist scientists must turn to one idea after another.

## What are some facts not explained by these "theories" on the origin of the solar system?

There are numerous problems that are not explained: (1) disproportionate angular momentum (the property that keeps the sun *rotating* and keeps the planets *revolving* around it); (2) marked deviation of smaller bodies from the "normal" type orbit; (3) rotation of Uranus and Venus on their axes in a direction that is opposite to planetary motion around the sun; (4) not all of the planetary satellites orbit their planets in the same direction; (5) the origin of the moon; and (6) heavier elements in the smaller planets.

## Do you believe that the universe was created in six twenty-four-hour days?

In the Bible we read, "In the beginning God created the heaven and the earth" (Gen. 1:1); "For in six days the LORD made heaven and earth, the sea, and all that in them is" (Exod. 20:11); "... for in six days the LORD made heaven and earth" (Exod. 31:17). I believe that any attempt to overlook the "evening and morning" cycle as twenty-four-hour days brings on great problems. I believe that the universe and everything in it was created in six twenty-four-hour days.

## What problems are raised by plants being created before the sun as recorded in the Genesis account?

This order of things results in real problems for those who give serious attention to the day-age concept, the idea that the days of Genesis were long periods of time. First, the motivation for proponents of the day-age concept centers in an uncritical acceptance of evolutionists' contentions that the earth is very old and acceptance of the geologic time scale. As shown previously, these ideas are not scientifically established. Second, plants created in the third day presumably depended on food produced by photosynthesis as we know it. Therefore radiant energy was necessary. Of course, the light created in the first day might have been a source of radiant energy for photosynthetic activity in the first plants.

Admittedly God has not given us all the answers. If He had, we would "be as gods." Again, I find the most direct meaning in Genesis 1 to be that of six, twenty-four-hour days. For this belief the assignment of the sun as a "timekeeper" on the next day after creation of plants presents no problems.

## What happened to the "theory" that the moon came from the earth?

Basically, it has been forgotten ever since the separation of the moon from the earth was shown to be a physical impossibility. At one time George Darwin, Charles Darwin's son, thought that the moon came from the earth, leaving the deep (approximately thirty-five thousand feet) trench off the Mariana Islands as the scar. I was taught this idea as a high school student. Today, young people are told that the moon and the earth are about the same "age." No one actually knows about the origin of the moon. Why is it so much larger than satellites of other planets and why does it have a much lower density than the earth if they supposedly had a common origin, as evolutionary astronomers try to maintain today?

## What does it mean that the world was made with an appearance of age?

I believe from all we read in the Bible that God made all things. To me this means that the entire universe was completely functional immediately as God spoke the various portions into being. By the end of the sixth day God saw that all was good, very good. There were land features, mature trees and other plants, mature animals, and mature human beings. They were fully functioning and thus would have had the "appearance of age." We see things now only somewhat like those beginning conditions. The effects of sin in the world and the Noachian Flood prevent any descriptions of original situations.

## COSMOLOGY AND COSMOGONY

### What is cosmology?

Cosmology is the science or study of the structure and motion of the universe as observable during the time of human existence. Cosmology includes the activities of astronomers that are directed at the study of stellar objects, their motions, and their interrelationships. Such studies depend upon the use of tools, instruments, and modern technology.

### What is cosmogony?

Cosmogony involves formulation of ideas on the origination and generation of the universe. It includes efforts to answer the question, Where did the universe come from? Such sets of ideas or models of the origin of the universe, however, do not qualify as *scientific* theories since no prior observations or test of predictions about origins are possible. Cosmogony is not the same as or included in cosmology.

## What about cosmogony according to the Scripture?

Genesis 1 and II Peter 3 contain God's examples of unchanging cosmogony. I believe that God knew that humankind, as His creation, would ask questions about first origins. Therefore the Bible contains in Genesis 1 and II Peter 3 basic cosmogonical thinking that remains unchanging and unchangeable. We can "know" even in the area of cosmogony.

## SPACE AND EXTRATERRESTRIAL LIFE

### How big is the universe?

No one knows the size of the universe. Although many men have tried to estimate its size, and some have concluded that it is finite and enclosed, others have concluded that the universe is infinite and without boundary. Infinity is a concept beyond complete comprehension by finite human beings. Astronomers fully admit that we do not know the geometry of the universe.

### Why do some creationists think that much of astrophysics* is "philosophy and vain deceit"?

This phrase from Colossians 2:8 might be given a great deal of thought these days as to its possible application to secularism, evolutionism, uniformitarianism, and in turn to insistent claims by astronomers that the universe (and thus all that is therein) came from an explosion of some dense particle. Since nothing can "prove" the basis of that system of thought, then proponents of the big bang "theory" will forever be faced with the question, Where did the dense particle that exploded come from in the first place? As has been well put by creationist scientists, the

---

*A branch of astronomy that deals with the physical properties of stars and planets and with the interaction between matter and radiation within a star or planet and in space.

starting point of any pattern of reasoning must be an established truth "outside" any given system of thought. Part of astrophysics centers in cosmogonical ideas of men designed to be consistent with a philosophy of naturalism. Therefore men's ideas and thoughts based on the "rudiments of the world, and not after Christ" can easily be seen as "philosophy and vain deceit," as when some men acknowledge no established truth "outside" their system of cosmogonical ideas. God's revelation in Genesis 1 and II Peter 3 is the established truth "outside" the limited, naturalistic ideas of finite human beings.

## What are some possible explanations of UFOs?

The following are possible explanations of UFOs offered by some cautious scientists: (1) natural objects misinterpreted, (2) deliberate hoaxes, (3) secret government projects, (4) psychological phenomena, (5) extraterrestrial vehicles. Except for the last one, these explanations seem quite plausible to me.

## Do you think that intelligent beings inhabit other planets or are present anywhere else in the universe?

When someone refers to "intelligent beings" somewhere else in the universe, I assume they refer to possible extraterrestrial life in the same form as we know human intelligent beings. Frankly, I do not know as a scientist whether there is life as we know it anywhere beyond the surface of the earth. Direct observation of the moon and indirect observation of Mars and Venus have resulted in negative findings. Thus there is no known life, at this time, anywhere else in the solar system. Of course one should have suspended judgment, but right now I do not believe God placed any intelligent life anywhere else than on this earth.

## What motivates evolutionists to search for life in space?

The idea of life on other planets fits in well with the belief of many leading scientists that life came to the earth from outer space. This is what I call the "cosmozoic" idea on the origin of life on the earth. Early proponents of the idea proposed that life was carried to the earth by meteorites. Some scientists claim that organic compounds have reached the earth via meteorites. But the evidence is disputable.

## Is it true that scientists expected a thick layer of dust on the moon?

At one time responsible scientists in the NASA program were hesitant about sending a human being to the surface of the moon. They reasoned that there would be a deep accumulation of meteoric dust (or "space dust") on the surface of the moon if the moon was as old as evolutionists claimed it to be. Some scientists fully expected at least several feet of such dust cover. Yet, direct observation by human beings clearly denied these expectations. The astronauts observed that the moon surface dust was only "scuff-deep." This was a good lesson about the need for direct checks of men's ideas where possible.

# 6

## Where Did Life Come From?

### ABIOGENESIS (SPONTANEOUS GENERATION) VERSUS BIOGENESIS

**What are the meanings of the terms *abiogenesis* and *biogenesis*?**

Abiogenesis is a synonym for spontaneous generation; that is, abiogenesis means life coming from nonliving matter. Similar terms have been used to refer to spontaneous generation of life at the submicroscopic level, such as neobiogenesis, biopoesis, and eobiogenesis. Using different names for spontaneous generation just adds to the confusion, not to the understanding. Biogenesis means life coming from living matter. In contrast to spontaneous generation, the law of biogenesis is a thoroughly documented law of biology.

**Did people once think that mature animals came into existence by spontaneous generation?**

Yes, ancient Greeks, Egyptians, and others thought that mature animals came into existence by spontaneous generation (life from nonliving matter). Aristotle maintained that fish, frogs, and mice could appear from such "breeding" materials as filth and moist soil. Mice were reported to appear spontaneously after floodings of the Nile River. Snakes were thought to have come from horses' hairs. And even Shakespeare had his leading characters in *Antony and Cleopatra, Julius Caesar,* and *Hamlet* tell about spontaneous generation of animals from materials such as moist mud, decaying hides and hair, and rotting meat.

At one time many people believed that flies came from putrifying meat. Francesco Redi, however, by using truly scientific methods, proved that flies come from immature stages (maggots) that appear on meat from eggs deposited there by flies. Redi was an early researcher who identified an excellent basis for the biological law that life comes from life. His experiment is usually described in biology textbooks.

## Did people once think that bacteria came into existence by spontaneous generation?

As experimental proofs increased against spontaneous generation of mature animals from nonliving matter, attention shifted to the belief that microorganisms appeared spontaneously. Several famous scientists supported the concept of spontaneous generation of microorganisms from organic particles, until the famous swan-neck experiments of Louis Pasteur in the nineteenth century. Pasteur won a prize for his successful experimentations by which he denied spontaneous generation of microorganisms. His work, in which he showed that bacteria came from bacteria, supported the law of biogenesis.

## Is evolution based upon belief in spontaneous generation?

Even after the splendid scientific experiments of Redi and Pasteur, the question still remained of how life on the earth started. Today many leading biologists clearly state their belief in spontaneous generation of life at the submicroscopic level of organization of matter. Dr. George Wald has often pointed out that the choice is between special creation of life or spontaneous generation of life. Evidently Dr. Wald and his evolutionist colleagues think that matter has a kind of inherent tendency to become organized in the presence of energy from some source such as lightning. Creationist scientists do not hesitate to point out that this is unscientific thinking and an attempt to explain the origin of first life in naturalistic terms.

## Where did God come from?

This is a question beyond all questions, and yet is asked most sincerely by young people pressing for application of scientists' basic assumption of cause and effect. If there is an effect there must be a cause or causes. The Bible does not provide an answer to this question. It simply affirms God's existence. Genesis 1:1 states, "In the beginning God. . . ." When God assigned Moses to lead the Israelites out of Egypt, Moses responded by saying that when he went to the people they would ask, "What is his [God's] name?" And God said to Moses, "I AM THAT I AM" (Exod. 3:14). In other words God is the Eternal One who has existed before all time—before the universe, before the earth, before all things.

## Is it proper to refer to "simple" living things?

Since the development and refinement of the electron microscope, no one can accurately refer to any living thing as "simple." There are single-celled organisms, such as amoeba and paramecia, but they are not simple, and should never have been considered as such. Limitations of observation resulted in some early investigators thinking that cells were composed primarily of cell membrane (and cell wall in plants), cytoplasm, and nucleus—hence they thought cells were "simple." Now, multiple organelles, little organs located within plant and animal cells, have been identified through use of the electron microscope. Hence all cells are complex.

## What are the mathematical probabilities of spontaneous generation?

Mathematicians and specialists in the theory of probability have given various answers to this question. Odds for the chance appearance of proteinlike molecules that are only building blocks of actual living substance are variously reported as being 1 in $10^{123}$ or 1 in $10^{320}$ or 1 in $10^{8373}$ or 1 in $10^{29345}$. Note that these figures apply to the chance appearance of nonliving molecules, not to single cells, or multicellular organisms. Evolution, or "amoeba to man," is truly impossible.

## Would ultraviolet light kill life substances that might form in the oceans?

A quiet ocean basin or some body of water near a volcano are favored sites for supposed first appearance of life according to evolutionist scientists. Yet they usually totally ignore the extremely destructive and damaging effect of ultraviolet light rays. Researchers have clearly shown that ultraviolet light penetration into ocean water would have easily destroyed any early beginnings of life such as that imagined by evolutionists.

## LIFE IN A TEST TUBE?

### Have scientists produced life in a test tube?

Biologists have synthesized amino acids in their test tubes; but they have not created life. It is true that scientists have taken methane, ammonia, and hydrogen and charged the mixture with electricity to produce amino acids. But amino acids are not alive. They are only building blocks of proteins. Just as scientists have *only synthesized* urea and rubber, they have *only synthesized* (but not created) the building blocks of living substance.

Of course, since success came from the application of human intelligence, such synthesis of amino acids did not occur by chance or spontaneously. Admittedly, there was an instantaneous reaction after scientists applied the electrical charge, but no scientist, by doing so, has initiated spontaneous generation of anything. By definition *spontaneous* means without any external intervention—and every scientist intervenes in every laboratory and every field investigation. Thus, by analogy, if human intelligence was required for synthesis of amino acids, then an intelligent Being, God the Creator, was the first cause of all things in the universe. We are without excuse for being unaware that the planning of God is evident in all things around us.

## LEFT-HANDED PROTEINS

### What is meant by the statement that all proteins in living things are left-handed?

In a manner of speaking, all protein substance in living things is composed of amino acids that are so structured around a main axis. This means that a combination of one part of carbon and three parts of hydrogen in one type of amino acid may be situated on the left or right side of the main axis. But only those varieties of the amino acids having the carbon and hydrogen combination on the left side of the main axis (left-handed) are found in proteins of living tissue. Even if a right-handed amino acid is introduced into a living organism, the organism will take the right-handed amino acid apart and make it over into a left-handed amino acid for use in protein production. (See chart, page 70.)

### If all proteins in living things are composed of left-handed amino acids does that mean that all things are related?

Evolutionists would say yes on the basis that things that are most similar are most closely related. This is only an assumption, however, and is contradictory to all genetic evidence of plant and animal breeding records. No genetic connection of any major kinds of plants or animals is known; no familial lineages can be demonstrated at all. Any basic similarity of all living things containing left-handed amino acids can realistically be seen as evidence of a common element of planning by God, the Creator. Again, all things were made by Him and for Him, and through Him all things consist—even all living organisms containing left-handed amino acids.

## DNA CODE AND MUTATIONS

### What is the DNA code?

This is a complex subject area and would require whole chapters to fully explain it. It may be sufficient to say here that DNA is an abbreviation of deoxyribonucleic acid, which is directly involved in the appearance of physical traits in living

# LEFT- AND RIGHT-HANDED AMINO ACID RESIDUES

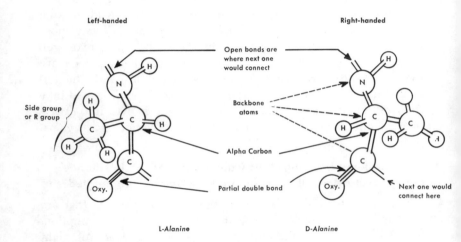

Left-handed                                                   Right-handed

Open bonds are where next one would connect

Side group or R group

Backbone atoms

Alpha Carbon

Partial double bond

Next one would connect here

L-Alanine                                   D-Alanine

Left- and right-handed amino acid residues. The molecules shown are L-alanine and D-alinine (L = levo, or left-handed; D = dextro, or right-handed). Alanine is the simplest of the amino acids which are isomeric or handed.

The bonds in the figure are not drawn to scale, but are lengthened so that the left- and right-handedness is more easily seen: In real molecules, the bonds are shorter so that the "surfaces" overlap, making the molecules more compact. The initials on the atoms indicate carbon, nitrogen, oxygen, and hydrogen. Note that the only difference between the two is the position of the side group, on either the left or right side.

70

organisms. Though partially identified and understood, the DNA code evidently is quite specific in organization for each kind of organism. (This fact might remind the reader of Paul's comment in I Corinthians 15:39, "All flesh is not the same flesh: but there is one kind of flesh of men, another flesh of beasts, another of fishes, and another of birds." What modern biochemists are finding out about DNA basically agrees that there is flesh of beasts, flesh of birds, flesh of fish, and flesh of man.)

## What is the "code" of the DNA code?

Applying the basic assumption of cause and effect so fundamental to scientific thinking, we are faced with the question that if the DNA code is causal to the appearance of physical traits, what was the cause of the formation of the DNA code? Of course evolutionists cannot answer this; it is another one of those great unanswerable questions. Geneticists are adding more and more details to their description of the DNA code for an increasing number of organisms, but, they cannot answer the question, What is the "code" of the DNA code? The creationist scientist maintains that the answer is that God the Creator originated the code.

## What are mutations? Are they the source of new physical traits?

Mutations are chance or random changes in the DNA structure—changes in genes (the units of inheritance). Mutations are *mistakes* because they commonly result from failure of cell functions, as best we understand to date, of duplication or copying of genic material. Ordinarily DNA materials are duplicated accurately in cells and each new cell contains DNA substances characteristic for the particular plant or animal involved. But sometimes proper duplication or copying does not occur—some mistake occurs in place of normal change—resulting in a mutation. Mutations can be passed from one generation to another as is seen in the appearance of such diseases as sickle-cell anemia, Tay-Sachs disease, and Huntington's chorea.

Yet mutations are *not* the source of any new physical traits.

71

Since they are the results of mistakes in duplication or copying of DNA material, mutations are nothing more than changes of already existing genes. Generally, mutations result in undesirable variations of already known physical traits.

## How important are mutations to evolutionary thinking?

Mutations are very important to evolutionary thinking. They have long been considered the "raw materials" for supposed evolutionary changes. When asked how changes like wings from nonwing or feathered from nonfeathered occurred, evolutionists respond in terms of slow accumulation of mutational modifications. For example, over enough time, scales might have become feathers.

Observations, however, are against such changes as the evolutionists imagine. The great preponderance of known mutations are deleterious, debilitating, or lethal and are not actually the source of any new physical traits. Further, there is no indisputable evidence of slow accumulation of mutational changes to the degree required for the evolutionists' ideas about common ancestry, for example, of all vertebrates. Although evolutionists fail to find any evidence, they imagine that wings, feathers, mammalian hair, eyes, upright walking posture, and other physical features came into existence in the past due to some mutational changes in previous organisms. The evidence, however, only shows variations of already existing physical traits.

## Is the genetic load increasing?

*Genetic load* refers to an increasing list of physical traits in human beings due to inheritance of one or more mutations. Geneticists fear that the gene complex of generation after generation of human beings will contain more and more undesirable traits, many of which are recessive—that is, expressible only when genes for these traits are double in an individual. This is one reason for broadening attention to genetic counseling clinics where presently understood principles of genetics may be explained to newlyweds and other couples desiring information about their possible offspring. After a lengthy study of family members of both male and female members of a pair of human beings, realistic predictions can be offered to help in decision making. A family physician can give information about genetic counseling clinics.

## RECAPITULATION AND EMBRYOS

### What is the "theory" of recapitulation? Do human embryos ever have gill slits? or tails?

The essence of the concept of recapitulation is that during development each embyro passes through abbreviated stages that resemble some developmental stage of a supposed evolutionary ancestor. This thesis has been thoroughly examined by modern biologists and found to be completely invalid.

Probably the two most widespread ideas associated with the concept of recapitulation are claims that human embryos have gill slits and tails at some stage of development. This is most certainly not the case. Although there are alternating ridges and grooves in embryos of mammals, birds, and reptiles, there are *never* any openings in these structures like gills. Actually, in mammals, the jaws, inner ear, tongue, tonsils, and other organs are formed from these ridges.

Occasionally a human baby is born with a protruding portion (coccyx) of the lower extent of the spinal column. This is because of incomplete formation of tissue around the lower end of the spine. The protruding part, however, is *not* a tail. Normally as the surrounding tissue develops, the protruding lower part of the spine is enclosed.

# 7

# Where Did Humankind Come From?

## HUMAN "EVOLUTION"

**Much is heard these days about "possible control of human evolution." What does this mean?**

This phrase does not suggest that some super being will come into existence from present human beings. What is meant by the phrase is possible directed changes *within* limits of humankind. Geneticists particularly are "exploring" ways of changing genes in human beings for a variety of objectives. This whole area of discussion is sometimes labeled "human engineering."

No matter how many objectives are realized or on what time schedule, human beings still will give rise to human beings. Hence genetic variation within kind is all that really can be anticipated. If the term *evolution* must be used, then the only proper term is that of *micro*evolution. But genetic variation within kind is much more expressive of the situation that prevails and will continue.

**How do evolutionists think human beings came into existence?**

Evolutionists believe that human beings evolved somehow from subhuman forms, such as Pliopithecus, Proconsul, Dryopithecus, Oreopithecus, and Ramapithecus. These are all imagined by evolutionists to be in the family history of humankind. Some evolutionists consider humankind most biologically related to the chimpanzee. There are points of similarity, but again, similarity is *not* a basis for establishing familial relationships.

74

Actually, genetic variation *within* limits very likely is all that has occurred in the past. Many evolutionary schemes, or evolutionary "trees," have been proposed in the time since the Neanderthal, Peking, and Cromagnon skeletons were found. But publication of evolutionary "trees" in no way establishes human beings as coming from any certain subhuman form.

At one time each of these forms was assigned to a separate genus. All these forms now, however, are placed in the genus *Homo*. Thus, today they are regarded primarily as different species of human beings along with *Homo erectus*. Much debate continues as to whether the Australopithecines were apes or human form.

### How do evolutionists account for the different races?

Races of humankind are accounted for primarily by invoking some type of serial changes by mutations. Supposedly a population of anthropoidlike organisms of possible olive shade was the "stock" from which different races of human beings mutated. Of course there is absolutely no observational information for such an imagined position. And there is also no clear consensus on the concept of "race." Nationalities and religious groups are not races. Anthropologists have used a wide range of physical characteristics to try to determine one race from another, but there are no clear lines of separation. *All* human beings belong to the same species *(sapiens)* of the same genus *(Homo)*, and all are potentially interfertile. The sound scientific position to maintain is that all human beings are human beings.

### How do creationists account for the different races?

As more and more scholarly work analyzing the early books of the Bible is completed, the evangelical believer is developing a confident position that the Bible contains actual history and is fully reliable. There is an excellent position of increasing authenticity of the Table of Nations in Genesis 10. Some fine work by anthropologist Dr. Arthur C. Custance, whose works are listed for your further reading (pp. 108-110), is basic to my own contention that all peoples of the earth alive today have come by long family relationship with the three sons of Noah: Shem, Ham, and Japheth. I commend the findings of Dr. Custance wherein he documents his position that God may well have had a three part economy for societal organization, and all present peoples on the earth came from families and nations named in the Bible.

### When did man appear on the earth?

This question, like the previous ones on the time life appeared on the earth and what the earth's "age" is, cannot be scientifically answered. Because of continued reliable archaeological work, scholars know that human beings were conducting complex economic and social functions close to six thousand years ago, and maybe some human beings were contemporary with the last stages of the so-called Ice Age (now commonly listed as ending about ten thousand years ago).

### Evolutionists stress similarites between anthropoids and human beings. What are some of the differences?

The most pronounced behavior difference is the two-part capacity of reflective awareness and *conceptual* thought that is part of the superior symbolic uniqueness of human beings. Only human beings are able to be completely independent of object stimuli in their conceptual thinking. Subhuman animals are stimulus-bound to direct or almost immediate presence of objects, and thus are limited to *perceptual* thinking only.

In physical terms human beings are different in their learned adaptability to changing environments and their unique, well-formed hand. Many soft body parts of the human being are different from subhuman animals. The place where the skull is attached to the spinal column is a very important physical difference. Skulls of human beings are attached to the spine near the center of the base of the skull; whereas skulls of subhuman anthropoids are attached to the spine near the back of the skull base.

## FOSSILS OF PREHISTORIC MAN

### Why have so few human skeletons been found?

This question is brought up often to challenge those who champion a world-wide flood interpretation of the Noachian Flood. It is reasonable to assume that human beings would have been most able to understand the consequences of the rising flood waters. They would have sought higher and higher ground. When they were finally overcome by the waters their bodies would have been on the surface and decomposition would have rapidly occurred. Skeletons that are being found in Africa, if skeletons of human beings, may well be evidence of individuals who were trapped by volcanic eruptions (similar to those of historical time destroyed by an eruption of Mount Vesuvius) and changes of the earth's surface as land masses settled into "balance" after retreat of flood waters. The Leakey family has conducted their prolonged search activities near major areas of rock movements due to earthquakes.

### How complete are the fossils of so-called prehistoric men?

Skeletal finds range from a femur bone, skull cap, or jaws with teeth in place to dozens of complete (or nearly complete) skeletons of Neanderthal-type people. For a long time the total collection of bones might have been just enough to fill two good-size suitcases. As research has continued skeletal parts have been found in many places in Europe, all around the Mediterranean Sea (particularly the Near East), Africa, China, and Java. Today numerous, complete fossil skeletons are known and new "finds" are often reported.

### How accurate are reconstructions of so-called ancestors of early man?

The whole matter of reconstruction is strongly influenced by evolutionists' preconceived ideas. No one *knows* what Neanderthal or Australopithecus actually looked like. For one Neanderthal skull different artists arrived at nine different reconstructions. All reconstructions are based on knowledge of bone structure, muscle patterns, and various functions of the body parts of human beings and other mammals, but the actual outward appearance becomes whatever the person doing the reconstructing *thinks* the outward appearance should have been. Reconstructions are risky, and the only fully reliable facts for scientific descriptions are the actual bones found in different locations.

## What is the significance of the geographic distribution of fossil prehistoric men?

Since skeletal remains of prehistoric men have been found in many places in Europe, all around the Mediterranean Sea (particularly in the Near East), Africa, China, and Java, some anthropologists have turned away from an evolutionary interpretation of ancestry. A migration-dispersal concept has been put forward since almost all prehistoric forms are placed in the same genus, *Homo,* in contrast to the situation about forty years ago when each was placed in a separate genus after being named by different discoverers.

The significance of the location of fossil sites of the prehistoric men might be that camps or cave locations of group activities have been found of peoples that migrated from the Tigris-Euphrates valleys, possibly contemporaneous with Abraham. These different groups of peoples could have become isolated and inbred in their removal from the main source of civilization that has long been assigned to the Near East—the Fertile Crescent of civilized human beings.

Of course this migration-dispersal idea contradicts the Leakeys' contention that the cradle of humankind was Africa. Further, the thought that all prehistoric forms were contemporaneous seems in stark contradiction to popularly accepted radioactive dates. There is much archaeological data, however, that the Leakeys cannot ignore, and the radioactive dates are only estimates. If skull 1470, one of Richard Leakey's finds, does represent a human being then it was contemporary with beings represented by skeletal finds that were supposedly ancestors to human beings according to evolutionists. More study is needed for the migration-dispersal concept, which is also discussed by Dr. Custance.

**Evolutionists now think that Neanderthal man walked upright. Why did they first represent Neanderthal with a stoop?**

Primarily because of their preconceived idea that human beings had to come from an animal origin. The ancestral forms imagined were characterized as somewhat intermediate between subhuman anthropoids and human beings. Also, decisions about appearance and behavior of Neanderthal were based on limited skeletal remains at first. As more samples were found, a different interpretation was necessary (that Neanderthal was in the same upright posture as modern man), especially when researchers found evidence that the first Neanderthal bones were diseased and thus the living individuals could have been deformed.

**Were Adam and Eve primitive cave people?**

My answer is influenced by my interpretation of Scripture that Adam, and in turn Eve made from Adam, were intelligent people. Adam knew how to name the animals. Somehow members of the early human family were instructed in speech and language by their Creator, and the beginning of agriculture, music, metallurgy, and other skills are fully indicated in the Bible as characteristic of early humankind.

**Was "Piltdown" man a "missing link"?**

The Piltdown "man" was not even a man, let alone a missing link." It is an example of the work of someone who believed in the supposed evolution of humankind so much that he was willing to commit a fraud. Sadly, the jaw from which Piltdown "man" (or "Dawn Man") was reconstructed had been filed, chemically treated to make it "old," and purposely buried where a search party would find it. The jaw was from a rather recent anthropoid.

**Did some evolutionists once try to make a man out of a pig's tooth?**

This question refers to *Hesperopithecus,* or Nebraska "man," which like Piltdown "man," was a figment of some men's imaginations. On the basis of too limited evidence and an overactive imagination, someone tried to reconstruct a prehistoric man out of a tooth of a peccary (piglike mammal). This is a good lesson on the need for caution, suspended judgment, and large amounts of skeletal materials before making extensive interpretations. The reserve of Dr. Richard Leakey with regard to his so human-like skull 1470 is commendable.

## DINOSAUR AND HUMAN TRACKS

### What is the significance of finding human footprints in the same rock layers as dinosaur footprints?

No fully conclusive evidence is possible but circumstancial evidence found in the Paluxy River near Glen Rose, Texas, southwest of Fort Worth challenges the evolutionists' claim that dinosaurs and human beings were separated by some seventy million years. Clear dinosaur tracks are found in Cretaceous limestone in the Paluxy River bed. Marks that look like human footprints in mud, fully analogous in size, stride, and movement dynamics, are found in the same sedimentary layers as the dinosaur tracks. According to this circumstantial evidence, human beings and dinosaurs were contemporary. Some research on the Paluxy River finds is documented in the film, *Footprints in Stone,* available from Films for Christ, N. Eden Road, Elmwood IL 61529.

### How do creationists explain dinosaurs? What caused their extinction?

Creationists believe that all things were made by God, including dinosaurs. There is no way of knowing what dinosaurs first looked like. Reconstructions of dinosaur skeletons must be viewed with the same skepticism that is recommended for reconstructions of human skeletons. Possibly the behemoth (or the leviathan) mentioned in the Book of Job were dinosaur forms. Dinosaurs may have been affected by the Curse, as many changes occurred at that time according to Scripture, and possibly "wiped out" at the time of the Noachian Flood. If they were taken on the Ark (maybe as young animals), they may have died as a result of climatic changes that occurred after a world-wide flood.

## WHAT DIFFERENCE DOES IT MAKE?

**What difference does it make whether human beings evolved or were special creations of an Almighty God?**

It makes a big difference, particularly with regard to how people react toward each other. Personal dignity, value, and worth are lost in viewing a human being as simply a made-over animal, another "evolved" member of a species. If a person sees another human being as God's creation, he realizes the individuality, personality, and uniqueness of that human being, as well as of himself. The personality of human beings can be understood as coming ultimately from God—who created all creatures, including humankind.

Belief in the creation of human beings by God provides a more fulfilling answer for the question, Who am I? You are a creation of a God who loves you and wants you to have full fellowship with Him by realizing yourself as His creation. This relationship is understandable to one who seeks to know his Creator, and removes the alienation and separation that results from belief in an "evolved" origin of humankind.

# 8

# What Is the Impact of Evolutionism?

## ADOPTION OF EVOLUTIONARY THINKING IN HUMAN KNOWLEDGE

### How widely has evolutionary thinking been adopted?

Today, evolutionary thinking has been adopted without question in every major discipline of human knowledge. This condition is the reverse of the "intellectual climate" when Charles Darwin was preparing for his famous voyage around the world on the H.M.S. *Beagle,* which began in 1831. At that time the predominant belief regarding origins was in favor of special creation.

The modern synthetic "theory" of evolution (a modification of Neo-Darwinism, which in turn was a modification of Darwinism) has been unquestionably adopted in economics, psychology, education, theology, philosophy, American history, political science, literature, and science. The enormity of this "capture" of the minds of such a wide range of intellectuals is seen as even more colossal when a candid inspection reveals the fact that megaevolution (amoeba to man) is *without any observational foundation.*

### What has been the impact of evolutionary thinking on the disciplines of human knowledge?

*Economics*

Karl Marx and Friedrich Engels, promoters of socialist thought, accepted Darwinism. These men wrote that Darwin had given them a biological basis for their identification of the so-called class struggle in society. They transferred the idea of struggle for existence, or survival of the fittest, from biology to society. Hence a "theory" of social evolution seemed to be a consistent extension of supposed biological evolution. Instead of species of organisms surviving, classes of workers were supposed to survive in competition with classes of industrialists. Extensions of Marx's thinking involving class warfare (excused as an extension of the struggle for existence that Darwin had made attractive to biologists and other intellectuals) can be traced in the writings of Beatrice and Sidney Webb in England, and in the works of John Maynard Keynes and his American followers as democratic socialism became established in the United States after 1932.

## Psychology

The impact of evolutionary thought on psychology can be traced to the acceptance of the concept of inheritance of acquired characteristics by Sigmund Freud. Inheritance of acquired characteristics (that characteristics acquired during the lifetime of an individual are transmitted to offspring) was fostered by Lamarck and used in the later edition of Darwin's *The Origin of Species.* Freud's acceptance of this idea, now fully discredited and completely rejected by biologists and geneticists, gave significant impetus to the environmentalist inclination so prominent in psychology. Acording to environmentalists, an individual's behavior is the consequence of the environment in which growth and development has occurred. Today, B. F. Skinner totally accepts the unscientific idea of the evolutionary origin of humankind. His thinking and writing is greatly beholden to the evolutionary viewpoint.

## Education

John Dewey, leading American educator, broadly accepted Darwinism. He supported the view that the human being was an "evolved" creature (slowly improving physically and mentally) and thus the environment in which schooling occurred became all important. Many, if not most, of Dewey's books stress the importance of evolutionary ideas. Because several generations of educators followed Dewey's thinking, environmentalism became a strong viewpoint in the development of educational principles and policies in the public schools in the United States.

## Theology

The broad acceptance of the Graff-Wellhausen "hypothesis" regarding criticism of biblical texts shows the impact of evolution on theology. Basically, the view is that the Bible content has "evolved." A most influential spokesman for this view of the "evolution" of the Bible was Henry Emerson Fosdick. He wrote about man's worship of God "evolving" from worship of a sun god and moon god, to a mountain god and river god, to a crop god, to a tribe god, to an Omnipotent God. The whole point of view of higher criticism and form criticism of the twentieth century is rooted in an evolutionary viewpoint.

## Philosophy

The impact of evolutionary thought on philosophy can be traced particularly to the broad application of criticism of nineteenth-century classification systems involving an archetype, a sort of creation kind. The evolutionists' position about supposed slow, gradual changes between organisms was mistakenly accepted as the basis for the attitude in philosophy that categories are not clearly defined, absolutes are not identifiable, and all things are relative (which of course is also traceable to interpretations of Einstein's thinking). Confusion in ethics and aesthetics was fostered by acceptance of evolutionary thinking in philosophy. The writings of John Dewey, who fully accepted evolutionary thinking, were also very influential in development of the "new" philosophy in the twentieth century.

## American History and Political Science

The impact of evolutionary thought on American history and political science can be traced as the thread of acceptance of

Karl Marx's thinking is examined. Marx used the struggle for existence concept which he found in Darwin's book, *The Origin of Species,* to support and excuse his thesis of class warfare. In American history this was continued by Charles A. Beard, who explained passage of the Constitution of the United States in each of the thirteen colonies as a result of class warfare (between the landed gentry and noblemen for the Constitution and farmers and the poor and indigent against the Constitution). His ideas were published in 1913, and not until forty years later Robert Brown and Forrest McDonald, two independent investigators, analyzed available colonial records (which Beard *never* did) and found Beard's thesis of class warfare in the colonies completely invalid.

In political science a similar impact of evolutionary thinking can be traced through analyzing the positions taken by Carl Becker and many others. Becker was quite evolutionary in his thinking and influenced several decades of graduate students—until he saw the logical consequences of the struggle for existence (in the form of the thesis that might makes right) when he studied the rape of Europe by Hitler's minions. There is no philosophical difference between Facist Germany and Communist Russia. The thinking of the leaders of the U.S.S.R. is deeply rooted in an evolutionary outlook. This is easily documented by tracing the acceptance of Marxism by Lenin and the eventual development of Bolshevism and Leninism.

*Literature*

Positions taken in the novels of Jack London, the plays of George Bernard Shaw, and even the poetry of Alfred Tennyson (who expressed an evolutionary viewpoint even before Darwin's book, *The Origin of Species*) provide a seemingly convincing basis for belief in the "evolution" of humankind (abetted by Darwin's second book, *The Descent of Man*).

Interestingly London and Shaw were both socialists in England, followers of the thinking of the Fabian Society, which came about from the work and efforts of Beatrice and Sidney Webb, who in turn were followers of Karl Marx. Both London and Shaw used their literary works to present socialistic views and illustrate the struggle for existence concept. London in particular popularized the "red tooth and claw" phrase through the struggles he wrote about in *White Fang* and *The Call of the Wild*.

## Science

The impact of evolutionary thought on science has been almost complete. However, weaknesses and deficiencies in Darwinism, Neo-Darwinism, and even the modern synthetic "theory" of evolution have been published by scientists in every decade since *The Origin of Species* was written in 1859. Yet such criticisms have not been included to any significant extent into science textbooks. Sir Julian Huxley, Theodosius Dobzhansky, and G. G. Simpson are examples of influential leaders of the infusion of evolutionary thinking in all facets of biology and associated sciences. Specific impetus inaugurated in the 1960s to expand and augment the teaching of evolutionary origins in the secondary schools in the United States was really an important cause of the development of creationism teaching, that is, explanation of the scientific basis for the creation account of origins.

**How might this broad impact of evolutionary thinking on the disciplines of human knowledge be represented diagrammatically?**

A picture is worth a 1,000 words; therefore the diagram on the opposite page is offered to summarize and highlight the "flow" of Darwin's influence. Again I want to mention the colossal scope of the "capture" of minds. Remember, megaevolution (amoeba to man) is *without any observational foundation*.

## TEACHING CREATION IN SCHOOLS

**Can you teach creation in your classes?**

I have been teaching a scientifically supported creation account of origins for over three years in my classes at Michigan

# THE "FLOW" OF DARWIN'S INFLUENCE

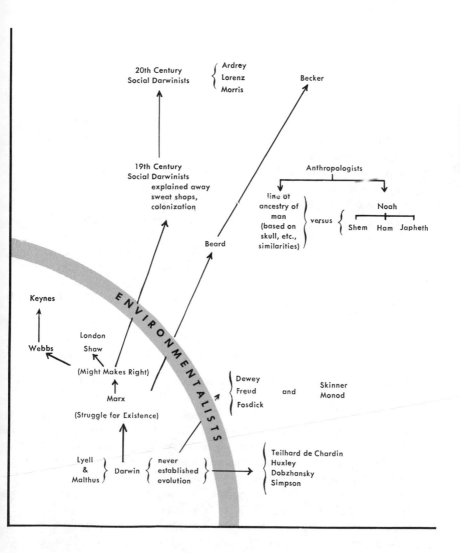

State University. This is done in accordance with full academic freedom and responsibility. I also teach the megaevolution (amoeba to man) thesis, noting the specifically circumstantial support.

**Is religion involved in teaching either creation or evolution?**

A large, unabridged dictionary defines "religion" as:
1. a belief in a divine or superhuman power to be obeyed and worshiped as creator and ruler of the universe;
2. an expression of this belief in conduct and ritual;
3. any specific system of belief, worship, or conduct.

I assure my students when I explain the creation model and evolution model of first origins that class work will not involve religion. By this I mean that *no worship* will be involved in class, *no special conduct* or ritual will be followed; that is, no prayer beads or prayer rug will be used, no facing the east, or worshipful conduct or ritual will be practiced. Hence no religion is involved in my classes.

I only give attention to the beliefs of men and women about the origins of the universe, life on the earth, and humankind since the creation model and evolution model are properly thought of as belief systems. These belief systems have been developed by their respective proponents to try to explain such questions as, Who am I? and Where did I come from?

**How do your students and colleagues react to your views?**

Ever since I began boldly announcing that a confrontation between the evolutionary viewpoint of the majority and the creation position of the minority would be sponsored in my classes, students have "over-subscribed" my classes at pre-registration time. Of course believers are reinforced and doubters find themselves really thinking about the live choice that I make so plain between the evolution model and the creation model.

In the last three years, my campus colleagues have recognized the substantive scientific basis of the creation account of first origins. I have given guest lectures, strictly upon invitation, to graduate students in zoology, honors section students in biology and botany, and students in the special science college. Departmental colleagues have opened their own lecture classes for a total of thirty presentations of a guest lecture, "A Scientific Case Against Evolution," in the same three-year period. They wanted their students to hear a concise, pointed, two-way presentation of the evolution model versus the creation model with regard to first origins. (Interestingly, colleagues involved have regularly been the younger instructors, with and without tenure.)

During the school year 1975/76 I was invited to make similar presentations to education methods students. I am now teaching two courses: a) my regular natural science course with an evolutionist colleague—we are both present in the lectures and discussion sessions to maximize confrontation before the students between proponents of the two basic viewpoints regarding first origins; and b) a special module elective on evolution vs. creation chosen by thirty-two senior education majors who have completed their student teaching.

In the pluralistic society of the United States of America indoctrination in the evolution model adopted by the majority is no longer necessary, nor can parents any longer allow their children to be so influenced to view themselves as made-over animals without some alternative. This selected indoctrination of young people at various levels of education regarding first origins of life and humankind must not continue. Because the megaevolution model and the creation model are put forth as conceptual frameworks to explain origins, science teachers are properly exercising their academic freedom and responsibility to present *both* the megaevolution model and the creation model to their students. On the grounds of constitutional and civil rights of students and science teachers alike, there are no significant reasons why other teachers in the United States and in other countries cannot do likewise for their students.

## What is the legal basis for teaching creation in the public schools?

No special ruling is needed. A straightforward consideration of the major viewpoints about first origins (evolution vs. creation) with students is fully within responsible edification of the young. This does not violate so-called separation of church and state. In fact, a sure way of guaranteeing that one pattern of beliefs is not favored over another is to assure fair treatment in a two-way fashion by at least teaching the evolution model versus the creation model regarding the origin of the universe, life, and humankind.

## Where does the teaching of evolutionary "theory" belong in the public schools?

Based on a strict point of view regarding the basic assumption of cause and effect, and since evolutionary "theory" involves questions of ultimate origins, all such discussion should ideally be considered a discussion in metaphysics. Therefore the teaching of evolutionary "theory" could be assigned to philosophy departments in colleges and universities. Most logically, then, the subject need not be touched in elementary and secondary schools.

Since, however, scientists do attempt to answer the questions of origins of the universe, life, and humankind, then science teachers seemingly should be duty bound in academic freedom and responsibility to present *both* the evolution model and the creation model.

## If creation is included in textbooks, must every other set of ideas about creation or origins be included?

Since beliefs on origins among other people have been derived from the Israelite-Hebrew tradition, passed orally for many generations and presented by Moses in Genesis, this is unnecessary. This position can be documented in scholarly research, but such study is beyond the scope of this book. See also pages 8 and 27.

## IMPORTANCE OF CREATION/EVOLUTION CONTROVERSY

## What is the importance of the creation-evolution controversy?

Fundamentally, the issue involved in the creation-evolution

controversy is a spiritual question. Is the individual in right relation with God the Creator—with Jesus Christ as Redeemer and Savior? For if Jesus Christ is not personally known as Lord, Master, and Creator of all things, then evolution, as amoeba to man, is the *only* basic substitute. Megaevolution becomes the philosophy and vain deceit designed after the ways of men and not after Christ, about which Paul warned Timothy—and all succeeding generations who would truly hear and know.

## Can science and the Scriptures ever really be separated?

Some have said that all facts are God-oriented—facts are either for God or against God. The triumph of Jesus Christ on the cross is the "watershed" of all time and existence—we still calculate historical time as B.C. (before Christ) and A.D. *(anno Domini,* "in the year of the Lord"). Even the facts of science have the fullest and most complete meaning as they are placed in an intellectually sound relationship to creative acts of Christ. Science began as an intellectual pursuit as a result of those men like Kepler, Newton, Clerk-Maxwell, and others who believed in God the Creator.

## Is atheism the logical consequence of the application of the "theory" of evolution?

The Communist educational structure, under the direction of declared atheists, definitely includes in the curriculum that human beings came from an animal origin. If humankind is not a special creation of God the Creator, then an animal origin is the only logical alternative. Nowhere does Scripture contain even a hint that God chose some anthropoid, some near man, and breathed the breath of life into it. With God all things are possible, and He breathed the breath of life into the dust of the earth. Naturalistically oriented atheists will not have God, so they must believe that humankind "evolved."

## Did any of the great scientists accept Christ?

I am always happy to answer this question in the affirmative. For many years, as a student and as a teacher before becoming a Christian, I did not know that Kepler, Newton, Clerk-Maxwell, and many other great scientists had accepted Jesus Christ as their Savior. Yet these great scientists declared in their writings and in their lives that they knew Christ and eternal life. In a sense these men were trying to think God's thoughts after Him. They believed that He created an orderly universe, which they could study to glorify God and gain dominion over portions of it as He had directed humankind to do. Such is nicely brought out in the high school textbook, *Physical Science for Christian Schools,* written in 1974 by Emmett L. Williams and George Mulfinger and published by Bob Jones University Press, Greenville, South Carolina 29614.

### What do you think of theistic evolution?

Theistic evolution is the position taken by so many modern people in intellectual likeness to the agnostics of the nineteenth century. I once thought theistic evolutionist thinking was acceptable. Yet it is only a compromise made by those who essentially value the viewpoint of men more than the unchanging message on origins contained in the Word of God. A theistic evolutionist thinks that God used evolution as a means for bringing into existence the great variety of life forms known today. A theistic evolutionist is more an evolutionist than a theist, since there is no observational basis that megaevolution (change from amoeba to man) has ever occurred. That evolution is without foundation is repeatedly observable in scientifically sound events. Therefore, there is no credible validity to thinking that evolution was God's way.

### If you were not a Christian, would you believe in evolution?

I would not believe in evolution even if I were not a Christian. I began to collect arguments by scientists against the megaevolutionary ideas for several years before I accepted Jesus Christ as my Savior. As details have been added I point out that belief in evolution is incredibly irrational. Is it rational to believe that all the orderliness of the universe came from an imagined explosion of a dense particle of absolutely unknown origin? Is it rational to believe that the first life on earth came from chance, spontaneous generation as molecular parts (also of unknown origin) supposedly combined into building blocks that became living substance that somehow became cellular? Is it rational to believe that humankind, which is the only life on earth (as far as we know) that is conscious of consciousness came from mutational changes (happy, fortuitous mistakes) that occurred in some subhuman form? To me, the answer to each of these questions is an unqualified no. Evolution is totally irrational.

## SOCIAL DARWINISTS

### Who were the nineteenth-century Social Darwinists?

After publication of Charles Darwin's book *The Origin of Species* in 1859, numerous people applied Darwin's ideas to human society. These people were called nineteenth-century Social Darwinists and included William Graham Sumner, John D. Rockefeller, Andrew Carnegie, Albert Galloway Keller, and Franklin H. Giddings, among others. They were either direct or indirect disciples of Herbert Spencer of England, who had popularized the phrase, "survival of the fittest." Early leaders in the then developing field of sociology and many industrialists used Spencer's phrase to explain away poor labor conditions and defeat of competitors as the result of a supposedly biologically founded law of competition. Spencer's phrase was most popular in the nineteenth century.

### Who are the twentieth-century Social Darwinists?

During recent years there has been a rebirth of Social Darwinism stimulated by a series of bestseller books authored by Robert Ardrey (a playwright), Konrad Lorenz (an anthropologist), and Desmond Morris (a zoologist). These speculative writers have done little, if any, research but try to persuade readers that human beings are genetically programmed for aggression and territoriality.

According to Ardrey, Lorenz, and Morris, human reactions are essentially of animal origin, since they assume a common evolutionary ancestry of human beings with other forms of life, especially anthropoid animals. These twentieth-century Social Darwinists present much speculation and long arguments built on analogies that are full of major flaws in logic and in knowledge of relevant data. They have failed to make a distinction between learned and instinctive behavior, between conceptual and perceptual thought, and between signs or signals and symbols.

A recent thrust in the direction of trying to explain human behavior basically in terms of genetic inheritance from animal origin is E. O. Wilson's book, *Sociobiology: The New Synthesis.* The author's position can be described as a mass of speculation and inconclusive anecdotes that likely will stimulate social resentments and controversy. Hopefully the new Social Darwinism will be rejected because of noticeable flaws and oversimplified thinking, as was the nineteenth-century version when rigorously analyzed.

## ADVICE TO PARENTS AND STUDENTS

### What is your advice to Christian parents and students involved with state educational institutions?

First and foremost, avoid argument with teachers in the classroom. Students who have done sound homework, however, who have studied the creation-evolution controversy, can make a real contribution to class activities. At the appropriate time students can ask definite, pointed questions, such as, What are the observational data for that conclusion? or What research does the author use to support his conclusion? This approach can stimulate classroom discussion and implement an opportunity for the informed student to help *all* concerned (fellow classmates and the teacher) to clearly perceive the problems involved. Academic freedom of all will be greatly enhanced.

Parents can purchase many supplementary reading materials for their school children regardless of the educational level: elementary, secondary, college and university, or even graduate level. Source addresses are given at the end of the section on further reading. Also, parents have opportunities to help teachers become aware of the increasingly significant creation science literature, published within the last ten years. Books could be given to teachers to evaluate. In such a manner extended discussions might follow. Parents could also be instrumental in placing creation science books in school libraries.

For those parents looking for real action, direct consultations with local school board members and members of the textbook evaluation committees of local school boards are recommended. In so doing parents can initiate the adoption of positive policies to encourage science teachers (and other teachers, when appropriate) to present a two-way approach to first origins through consideration of the creation model *and* the evolution model.

# Appendix One

Summary of Major Points
Covered in This Book

This book was designed as a collection of typical question and answer exchanges after public lectures, seminars, and special classes in which I have participated. This collection is not exhaustive, but is representative of pertinent problem areas of most interest to students, parents, and pastors. I pray that these questions and answers on creation and evolution will be used by the Holy Spirit to strengthen and edify many Christians who are firm in their relation to God through Jesus Christ as born-again believers. Further, I trust that other readers will be stimulated and challenged to consider all the points they encounter in these pages and to reconsider all evolutionary ideas they may have held when they began reading this book.

In summary, I offer the following listing of condensed statements relevant to each chapter area:

1. Observation, plus repeated observation, is at the very center of precise scientific activity. Therefore, since ideas formulated about the origin of the universe, the origin of life, and the origin of humankind involve unobservable, unrepeatable events, then those ideas are outside precise scientific activity.

2. Precise scientific activity is restricted to empirical, quantitative, mechanical, and correctable studies.

3. Most commonly, evolution is understood to mean "molecules to man," or "amoeba to man," changes.

4. Most modern creationists believe that all that is in the heavens, on the earth, and in the seas originally came into existence by the creative acts of God the Creator.

5. If first origins are presented in any course then a two-way treatment of concepts of the creation model and the evolution model is required to protect the academic freedom and civil and constitutional rights of all persons involved in the educative process.

6. The terms *kind* and *species* are difficult to define but are not equivalent. Possibly "created kind" could refer to arbitrary classification divisions of order, family, or genus.

7. All scientists use the same main categories of evidence, but the evidences are interpreted differently: the proponents of the evolution model emphasize *similarities,* whereas proponents of the creation model emphasize *differences.*

8. The entire system of evolutionary thought rests upon the basic assumption that the degree of relationship depends upon the degree of similarity.

9. There are two degrees of change that must always be made explicit when discussing origins of plants and animals: (a) change *within* recognizable kind of organism, which is most adequately called "genetic variation" (within kind); and (b) supposed change *across* recognizable kind, which is appropriately called megaevolution or macroevolution (amobea to man).

10. There is a "fixity of kinds" that may be supported conclusively from plant and animal breeding records. This phrase could well be the twentieth-century equivalent to the biblical phrases "after his kind" or "after their kind."

11. There are no compelling scientific grounds for maintaining that the earth (or the universe) is billions of years old. All proposed methods of dating only result in estimates of age. There are sound reasons for claiming that the earth and the universe are young.

12. Each of the adopted radioactive dating processes are based on limiting assumptions. No one can determine initial

ratios of elements when the earth began, nor whether decay rates have always remained constant.

13. There are no compelling scientific reasons for assuming that the days of the creation week in Genesis 1 were anything but twenty-four-hour days.

14. The complete geological column utilized by many geologists to estimate the age of rock strata and fossils in rocks does not exist anywhere on the surface of the earth.

15. Since sedimentary rocks are the most widely distributed rocks at or near the surface of the earth, and since geologists interpret that such rocks were formed after rock fragments and sediments accumulated under water, there is abundant circumstantial evidence for a world-wide flood (such as most creationists interpret the Noachian Flood).

16. Though uniformitarian geologists refer repeatedly to the concept that the present is the key to the past, they regularly imagine forces regarding mountain building, mountain range erosion, and continental glaciation that are unobservable. Uniformitarian geologists, therefore, really include supranatural events in their thinking, and hence contradict their own desire to refer only to events which occur naturally.

17. There are no known intermediate or transitional forms with genetic connections between recognizable kinds of plants and animals in the fossil record.

18. The concept of "fixity of kinds" can be supported by a long list of "living fossils," organisms once thought to have been extinct but now known to be alive.

19. Concepts of overthrust of rock layers over other layers can be applied in very restricted regions but not for major areas as in Glacier National Park and in the Alps.

20. Actual movement of the continents occurs according to data available today, but the idea of an original land mass (called Gondwannaland by some) will always be a matter of speculative fiction and cannot be checked by present technology.

21. Noah's ark was quite large enough to have carried all the different *kinds* of animals.

22. Attention must regularly be called to the empirical nature of cosmology and the highly speculative, imaginative nature of cosmogony.

23. Considering that the heavens and the earth and the seas and everything in them were created by God in six days and that He found it all good, it seems most logical that all things were fully functional and would have had the appearance of age.

24. Conceptual formulations of "big bang" expansion and steady state existence of components of the universe are examples of nonscientific speculative (imaginative cosmogonal) thinking outside the scope of empirical and theoretical activities of scientific work.

25. Some scientists still believe that life came into existence by spontaneous generation, that is, by a chance coming together of submolecular parts of matter.

26. Life is known only in complex organization, though admittedly in single cell (as well as multiple cell) patterns, but never in simple form.

27. Evolution (molecules to man) is mathematically impossible and really quite irrational. The fact that proteins in living things are composed only of left-handed amino acids compounds the problem of credibility of evolutionist thinking.

28. All efforts directed at producing living material in the laboratory utilize already existing materials, and thus synthesis, rather than creation, is involved.

29. If scientists are ever successful in producing synthetic living substance, then they will have demonstrated that intelligent planning was involved; hence, by analogy, an Intelligence (God the Creator) was responsible for the initial pattern of organization of first life on the earth.

30. Though physical features of plants and animals may well be due to the DNA code, there is no known "code" of the code

to explain how the patterns of the DNA codes found in plants and animals first came into existence.

31. Mutations do not result in any new physical traits, but only in characteristically variational changes of known physical traits. Usually mutational changes result in debilitating conditions, loss of viability, or death.

32. At no time do human beings ever have any functional tails or gills. Any claims for the existence of such features are based on abnormal conditions during development of an individual that usually disappear.

33. No known anthropoid ancester of human beings is known. There are pronounced differences between human beings and any form of animal life.

34. Reconstructions of so-called prehistoric men have really been the result of preconceived ideas that human beings came from some anthropoid origin.

35. Some anthropologists have turned away from an evolutionary interpretation of human ancestry and now propose that the widely scattered, so-called prehistoric fossil forms might have been isolated, inbred migrants from a Near East center of civilization.

36. Some circumstantial evidence has been found in the Paluxy River area of Texas that dinosaurs and human beings might have been contemporaneous.

37. Significant consequences of belief in an evolutionary ancestry of human beings instead of descent from an original created pair (Adam and Eve) are the lack of identity and the problem of explaining the source of human personality.

38. The concept of evolutionary origin of humankind has been accepted in every major discipline of human knowledge. The broad scope of such acceptance is specific evidence of the multiple impact of the totally unobservable, undemonstrable evolution model of origins.

39. Teaching the creation model versus the evolution model of origin is the only direct guarantee that selected indoctrination

during first origin instruction will be avoided. Such teaching about different beliefs of first origins is fully consistent with Supreme Court rulings concerning teaching about beliefs of different people.

40. Fundamentally the issue involved in the creation-evolution controversy is a spiritual matter. Is the individual in right relation with God the Creator, with Jesus Christ as Redeemer and Savior?

41. Serious misapplications of evolutionary thinking in the nineteenth century were practiced by Social Darwinists, and numerous examples of similar misapplications are committed today by twentieth-century Social Darwinists.

# Appendix Two

## DEFINITIONS OF SCIENTIFIC TERMS

**Assumption:**
**(Postulate)**
a statement of a concept taken for granted and not tested during particular scientific activity (explicated as basic assumptions, experimental assumptions, or theoretical assumptions).

**Basic assumption:**
**(Presupposition)**
a statement taken for granted as an untestable given upon which scientific activities (and intellectual discourse) are based such as:
1. Objectivity of study is possible.
2. Objects and/or events exist independent of observers.
3. Cause and effect relationships exist that may be identified.
4. Scientific ideas are testable, i.e., falsifiable, or not.
5. There is uniformity in the natural environment.

**Fact 1:**
an object and/or event in space at some time.

**Observation:**
a written or spoken record (as communication to self or another) of an awareness (perception) of an object and/or event.

**Description:**
**(Fact 2)**
a statement about some object and/or event in space-time. *(This is the lowest [basic] level of scientific explanation.)*

**Classification**
the end result of ordering of objects and/or events according to stated criteria.
—or the process of ordering objects and/or events according to stated criteria.

**Calculation:**
some arithmetic and/or mathematical manipulation of abstract and numerical symbols.

**Problem:**
an interrogation or stated perplexity for which an answer is sought. (A problem is most properly expressed in question form.)

# Appendix 2

**Hypothesis:** a tentative answer to a problem. (A hypothesis is most properly expressed as an assertive statement in form suitable for testing.)

**Analogy:** an expression or comparison of like or similar aspects of known objects, events and/or ideas, concepts.

**Generalization:** a statement of common aspects of similar objects and/or events.
—or an assertion that something is true about all members of a certain class of objects and/or events.

**Scientific law:** a repeatedly tested and well-supported or substantiated generalization of seemingly universal application regarding a certain set of facts (a level of scientific explanation between description and scientific theory).

**Prediction:**
**(Expectation)** that expected or projected state of affairs or relationship of objects and/or events based upon known or understood conditions; often found in an if . . . then expression.

**Experiment:** a specifically designed use of equipment, tools of measurement, and controlled variable components to gain observations and descriptions usually otherwise unobtainable.

**Experimental**
**assumption:** a statement about that aspect(s) of experimentation (controlled or of trial-and-error category) that is taken for granted as "noncritical" and not measured in any way.

**Cosmology:** the study of the nature of the universe; use of tools and technology to describe aspects of the observable and physical universe.

**Explanation:** a particular frame of reference used to provide meaning for particular facts. (Something has been "explained" when the statement, "I understand," can be made in response to the explanation offered.)

**Scientific theory:**
**(such as molecular-**
**kinetic theory, mod-**
**ern atomic theory,**
**nuclear theory,**
**gene theory)** a list of postulates or assumptions (theoretical) usually specifying existence, relationship, and events concerning an imaginary entity (such as an atom, gene, or molecule) whereby a meaningful "explanatory system" for a range of rather diverse facts is made available. Postulates are based upon prior observations of relevant objects and/or events; and, in turn, are bases of predictions testable by experience, directly or indirectly. (This is the highest level of scientific explanation.)

**Theorem:** a statement derived from assumptions of scientific theory more or less in the form of testable predictions or expectations.

**Model:**
a physical object designed to show analogical representation of some larger object(s) and/or event(s).

—or a conceptual pattern involving listed statements about imaginary objects and/or events and supposed relationships, especially associated with concepts of origination and generation.

**Cosmogony:**
a list of ideas or formulations centered on origination and generation of the universe. (Such conceptual patterns or models do not qualify as scientific theories since no prior observations or testable predictions about origins are possible.)

**Evolution model:**
an explanatory belief system based upon eternal existence of matter from which have come an ascending series of elements by nucleogenesis, changes by stellar evolution of "young" stars into "old" stars, galaxies, planets—especially the earth with life that appeared spontaneously through molecular evolution followed by organic evolution, including human evolution. (Ideas have to do with *origination* of order out of disorder and *integration* of more complex patterns out of least complex patterns.)

**Creation model:**
an explanatory belief system based upon existence of an eternal Creator who established a completed, finished, and functional universe in all aspects regarding elements, galaxies, stars, planets—especially the earth with mutually exclusive groups of animals and plants. (Ideas have to do with *conservation* of known conditions; yet, changes of *decay* and *degeneration* are evident and easily documented.)

**Science:**
an interconnected series of concepts and conceptual schemes that have been developed as a result of experimentation and observation and are fruitful of further experimentation and observation.

—or the body of knowledge obtained by methods based upon the authority of observation. (Science is limited to the study of nature; that is, study of matter and energy, because of limiting principles of being empirical, quantitative, mechanical [materialistic], and corrective.)

**Scientism:**
the belief that the only knowledge of repute and value is that obtained by means of the scientific process.

—or the belief that there is nothing but nonintelligent matter and energy.

**Technology:**
the totality of the means employed by peoples to provide material objects for human sustenance and comfort.

# Appendix Three

## EXAMPLES OF SCIENTIFIC ACTIVITY

### Examples Regarding Empirical Aspects of Scientific Activities

No scientist begins any experiment or field study without first having noted certain aspects of his or her environment that stimulated curiosity and the desire to learn more facts. So anyone interested in the life cycle of insects or even movements of planets and comets has made some sort of *prior observations* before starting serious, directed scientific study.

These prior observations are usually recorded initially as *descriptions* of observed aspects of objects and/or events of which the investigator has become aware. So the scientist would have noted the flight of insects, seen caterpillars, and maybe collected several cocoons; all of which he would group or order so as to associate these initial observations with insects—an important group in animal *classification*. Or an astronomer, the scientist most interested in stars and planets, may have initially observed planetary motions and formed a classification of "inner planets" and "outer planets" with respect to his description of their positions and the sun as center of the solar system. Each scientist would reasonably be expected to make numerical *calculations*, such as weight or length or period of rotation, as would be appropriate for the chosen area of empirical study.

On the basis of initial observations, descriptions, classifications, and calculations a scientific researcher would next formulate carefully stated *problems*, that is, specific questions for which answers would be sought within the limits of available tools and instruments of investigation. Because tools and instrumentation have been improved century after century both physical scientists and biological scientists have been able to scientifically study an increasingly wide range of problems and questions.

The real genius or "art" of the scientist is shown in the type of *hypotheses*, or tentative answers, that are formulated after scientific problems have been recognized. Scientific curiosity is channeled most successfully and profitably for the benefit of humankind when *testable* tentative answers (in the form of hypotheses) to problems are formulated. Quite often *analogy* is involved as comparisons between known or well-understood phenomena and unknown objects and/or events are worked out. For instance, comparison of the human body and the internal combustion machine has been a helpful analogy. (The human body is *not* a machine, but one can accurately state that the human body is machinelike, since raw materials are utilized, energy is released, by-products are formed, and waste products are released.)

The entomologist (a scientist who studies insects and their life cycles) might formulate a testable hypothesis as he tries to solve problems—questions such as: How long does a single insect live?, How many eggs are laid by a female insect?, What stage appears next after the egg?, or What are the various stages of metamorphosis? And the astronomer might formulate a testable hypothesis as he tries to solve the problems, How many moons are associated with a given planet?, How often does a planet rotate, or How many phases of Venus are there?

Methods of testing hypotheses will vary and can range from simple trial-and-error studies to tests of logical reasonableness and internal consistency to complicated controlled experiments. In controlled experiments certain aspects of the field of study vary or are allowed to change while other aspects are held constant or unchanging. Thus new facts can be gained that would not have been observed without the controlled experiment.

As all the observations, descriptions, calculations, and new facts gained from testing hypotheses are accumulated, scientists look for patterns so that they can state a *generalization,* which is a notation of common aspects of similar objects and/or events. Certain common or similar points would have become evident to the entomologist as he studied insects, or to the astronomer as he studied planets, and hence summary statements could be expected in the form of generalizations about the common or similar aspects of insects and planets, respectively. Those generalizations that are well supported or substantiated by extensive and repeated observations and testing are often accepted as *laws,* such as Boyle's law on gases, or Mendel's laws on inheritance.

## Examples Regarding Theoretical Aspects of Scientific Activities

Though empirical scientific activities are basic to all proper scientific work the crowning achievement of scientists is the development of broad, inclusive explanations, which are most appropriately called *scientific theories* (theoretical models or conceptual schemes). In contrast to generalizations and laws, scientific theories are useful means of interrelating or correlating widely diverse and seemingly unrelated facts. For instance, the gene theory relates facts of inheritance of a wide range of plants and animals.

Most simply, a scientific theory is a list of *postulates* (or theoretical assumptions) about the existence of some imaginary object or event, such as atoms, molecules or genes. Examples of postulates of scientific theories are as follows:

## Appendix 3

**Postulates of the Gene Theory:**

1. Genes normally exist in pairs per trait in zygotes, body cells, and gonadal generative cells.
2. Only one gene per trait normally exists in gametes.
3. Two genes exist per trait normally in a zygote after fertilization.
4. One gene may be dominant to another gene.
5. Gene pairs may combine randomly and independently during gamete formation and as a result of fertilization.
6. A series of genes may influence the same trait.
7. More than one gene are located on a single chromosome.
8. Exchange of genes is possible as exchange of chromosome parts occurs.
9. More than one pair of genes may influence the same trait.

**Postulates of the Nuclear-Electron Theory:**

1. An atom is composed of nucleus surrounded by a cloud of electrons.
2. The nucleus is composed of protons and neutrons.
3. The proton has a positive charge.
4. The electron has a negative charge.
5. The number of protons equals the number of electrons.
6. The number of positive charges on a nucleus is called the atomic number.
7. Neutrons are uncharged particles which still have mass.
8. The atomic weight of an element is the sum of the number of protons and neutrons in the nucleus.
9. Atoms of an element may have the same atomic number but different atomic weights (isotopes).

Postulates are typically worded so as to describe the existence, behavior, or interrelationship of such imaginary objects as genes or atoms. From the list of postulates scientists deduce *theorems* (or *predictions)* about unknown aspects of behavior or organization of the postulated imaginary genes or atoms. Such theorems should be testable. Because of the logical consistency and deductive reasoning applied to the gene concept and the gene theory, geneticists (scientists who study inheritance of physical traits and characteristics in plants and animals) now know that many genes affect the same trait. This is an example of the modifiable nature of the scientific gene theory, inasmuch as early geneticists thought that each physical trait was caused by a single gene.

Many more examples could be given of the fruitfulness of the gene theory as generative of more knowledge of inheritance. Thus the double-headed arrow in the chart of *Aspects of Scientific Activities* is exemplified. All proper scientific theories are based upon empirical aspects of scientific activity and, in turn, scientific theories are fruitful of further observation and experimentation.

Of course all empirical and theoretical aspects of scientific activity are based upon the fundamental, basic assumptions as listed. Actually such assumptions underlie all intellectual activities in the communicative arts, natural sciences, social sciences, and the humanities.

# Recommended Books and Periodicals for Further Reading

## Books and Periodicals

Barnes, Thomas G. *Origin and Destiny of the Earth's Magnetic Field.* San Diego: Institute for Creation Research, 1973.

Bliss, Richard B. *Origins: Two Models.* San Diego: Creation-Life, 1976.

Clark, R. T. and Bales, James D. *Why Scientists Accept Evolution.* Nutley, N.J.: Presbyterian & Reformed, 1966.

Coppedge, James. *Evolution: Possible or Impossible?* Grand Rapids, Mich.: Zondervan, 1973.

Culp, G. Richard. *Remember Thy Creator.* Grand Rapids, Mich.: Baker, 1975.

Custance, Arthur C. *Genesis and Early Man.* Grand Rapids, Mich.: Zondervan, 1975.

———. *Noah's Three Sons: Human History in Three Dimensions.* Grand Rapids, Mich.: Zondervan, 1975.

———. *Evolution or Creation?* Grand Rapids, Mich.: Zondervan, 1976.

Davidheiser, Bolton. *Evolution and Christian Faith.* Nutley, N.J.: Presbyterian & Reformed, 1969.

Friar, Wayne and Davis, P. William. *The Case for Creation.* Rev. ed. Chicago: Moody, 1972.

Gish, Duane T. *Speculations and Experiments on the Origin of Life.* San Diego: Institute for Creation Research, 1972.

———. *Evidence Against Evolution.* Wheaton, Ill.: Tyndale, 1972.

———. "Creation, Evolution, and the Historical Evidence," *American Biology Teacher,* March 1973, pp. 132-41.

————. *Evolution, The Fossils Say NO!* 2d ed. San Diego: Institute for Creation Research, 1973.

Howe, George F., ed. *Speak to the Earth: Creation Studies in Geoscience.* Nutley, N.J.: Presbyterian & Reformed, 1975.

Klotz, John W. *Genes, Genesis and Evolution.* St. Louis: Concordia, 1970.

Kofahl, Robert E. and Segraves, Kelly L. *The Creation Explanation.* Wheaton, Ill.: Harold Shaw, 1975.

Lammerts, Walter E., ed. *Why Not Creation?* Nutley, N.J.: Presbyterian & Reformed, 1970.

————. *Scientific Studies in Special Creation.* Nutley, N.J.: Presbyterian & Reformed, 1971.

Lester, Lane P.; Anderson, Wyatt W.; Moore, John N.; and Simpson, Ronald D. "Evolutionist-Creationist Roundtable," *The Science Teacher,* November, 1976, pp. 34-39.

Macbeth, Norman. *Darwin Retried: An Appeal to Reason.* New York: Dell, 1973.

Moore, John N. "Evolution, Creation, and the Scientific Method," *American Biology Teacher,* January 1973, pp. 23-26.

————. *Should Evolution Be Taught?* San Diego: Creation-Life, 1974.

Moore, John N. and Slusher, Harold S., eds. *Biology: A Search for Order in Complexity.* Rev. ed. Grand Rapids, Mich.: Zondervan, 1974.

Morris, Henry M. *Biblical Cosmology and Modern Science.* Grand Rapids, Mich.: Baker, 1970.

————. *The Troubled Waters of Evolution.* San Diego: Creation-Life, 1974.

————. *The Genesis Record.* Grand Rapids, Mich.: Baker, 1976.

Morris, Henry M., ed. *Scientific Creationism.* San Diego: Creation-Life, 1974.

Riegle, David D. *Creation or Evolution?* Grand Rapids, Mich.: Zondervan, 1971.

Siegler, H. R. *Evolution or Degeneration Which?* Milwaukee, Wis.: Northwestern, 1972.

Slusher, Harold S. *Critique of Radiometric Dating.* San Diego: Institute for Creation Research, 1973.

Smith, A. E. Wilder. *Man's Origin and Man's Destiny*. Wheaton, Ill.: Harold Shaw, 1968.

———. *The Creation of Life*. Wheaton, Ill.: Harold Shaw, 1970.

Whitcomb, John C., Jr. *The Origin of the Solar System*. Nutley, N.J.: Presbyterian & Reformed, 1964.

———. *The Early Earth*. Grand Rapids, Mich.: Baker, 1972.

———. *The World That Perished*. Grand Rapids, Mich.: Baker, 1973.

Whitcomb, John C., Jr., and Morris, Henry M. *The Genesis Flood*. Nutley, N.J.: Presbyterian & Reformed, 1961.

Wysong, R. L. *The Creation-Evolution Controversy*. East Lansing, Mich.: Inquiry Press, 1976.

Zimmerman, Paul A., ed. *Darwin, Evolution and Creation*. St. Louis: Concordia, 1959.

———. *Creation, Evolution, and God's Word*. St. Louis: Concordia, 1972.

## Recommended Periodicals

*Acts and Facts*. Monthly. Institute for Creation Research. San Diego, California.

*Creation Research Society Quarterly*. Creation Research Society, Ann Arbor, Michigan.

## Recommended for Parental Attention

"Action Manual: For Correcting the Imbalance in Education, Especially in Regards to Origins." Creation-Science Research Center, 6709 Convoy Court, San Diego, CA 92111. (Free)

Educational Research Analysts, M. F. Gabler, Box 7518, Longview, TX 75601. Source of excellent textbook analysis information. (See also *Textbooks on Trial* by James C. Hefley. Wheaton, Ill.: Victor Books, 1976.)

"Introducing Scientific Creationism into the Public Schools" by Dr. Henry M. Morris. 1975. Creation-Life Publishers, Box 15666, San Diego, CA 92115. ($.30 each, $25 per 100 copies.)

"Our Beautiful World" (a weekly science reader for nursery-kindergarten). Also "Our Wonderful World" (for grades 1-3), "Our Orderly World" (for grades 4-6), and "Our Scientific World" (for grades 7-9). Bible-Science Association, Box 1016, Caldwell, Idaho 83605. (Individual subscriptions at $1.50, $2.50, $3.00, and $3.50 per year, respectively. Large order rates available.)